INTERNATIONAL HAND ALPHABET CHARTS

second edition

edited and compiled by

Simon J. Carmel

Published by the Author

1982

INTERNATIONAL HAND ALPHABET CHARTS

Second Edition

Cover designed by DAVID LEIGH
Many illustrations by GENE FELTON

Also by Simon J. Carmel

International Hand Number Charts (forthcoming)

Copyright © Simon J. Carmel 1975, 1982

First printed in the United States of America
by
Studio Printing Incorporated
Rockville, Maryland 20851, U.S.A.

Library of Congress Catalog Card Number 81-90361
ISBN 0-9600886-2-8

To all the deaf people of the world
and their hearing friends

CONTENTS

HAND ALPHABET CHARTS

Countries

HAND ALPHABET CHARTS FOR THE DEAF-BLIND

Appendices:

FOREWORD

One of the most heartening developments in the United States over the last decade has been the proliferation of instructional books and manuals on the sign language of the deaf. The movement reflects the attitudes and concerns of today's society regarding the barriers of communication which, for too long, have separated the deaf from the hearing. As the poet, Robert Frost, so sagely observed: "Something there is that doesn't love a wall . . . that wants it down."

This book, then, is an attempt to breach the "Wall of Silence" and bridge the communication gap. It also offers the most simplified method of communication between the deaf and hearing, namely, the manual alphabet. Fingerspelling is still the quickest and easiest method for hearing persons to learn; it is the basic tool for instant communication. This is substantiated by the fact that fingerspelling provides the most accurate and effective mode of communication with the deaf-blind, as the experience of Helen Keller so vividly demonstrates. It is further evidenced in the world wide dissemination of the manual alphabet in the many and various publications read by "The Family of Man", such as in encyclopedias, household almanacs, books of knowledge, and the Boy Scouts of America *Handbook*.

The book should also provide a viable channel of communication for the adult deaf as they daily become aware of the diminishing perimeters of our small planet. Deaf people from all over the world are beginning to travel to different countries to attend international affairs for the deaf, such as the World Summer and Winter Games for the Deaf, the World Federation of the Deaf Congress, and the International Congress on Education of the Deaf. Along with their *Baedeker,* this handbook of manual alphabet charts should offer a ready means of communication with their fellow deaf in referring to *person, places,* and *things.*

Finally, it may be of great assistance to those under-developed countries which have need to develop their own manual alphabet charts for the continuing education of deaf children and adults. Two prime examples are the hand alphabets of Israel and Iran, which were devised in 1974 as the result of linguistic research by the author and several collaborators.

Simon Carmel is to be commended for his feat of interweaving these threads to form the fabric of this pioneering work. It is another milestone in his vita, which, among other achievements, includes a successful career as a physicist in the National Bureau of Standards (Washington, D.C.); President of the U.S. Deaf Skiers Association, which he also organized; General Chairman of the U.S. Organizing Committee of the American Athletic Association of the Deaf for the 8th World Winter Games for the Deaf at Lake Placid, New York in February, 1975; and an inveterate globe-trotter.

His latest venture into anthropolinguistics invites us to join hands around the world and build better bridges to communication.

Robert F. Panara
Professor of English & Drama
National Technical Institute
for the Deaf
Rochester Institute of Technology
Rochester, New York

PREFACE TO SECOND EDITION

Six years have passed since the first edition of *International Hand Alphabet Charts* was published. The purpose is the same for the second edition as for the first: to gather in one place as many as possible of the manual alphabet codes of deaf people world wide.

This edition contains hand alphabet charts for the following countries or areas not included in the first edition: Chile, Costa Rica, Egypt, Ethiopia, Iceland, India, Indonesia, Paraguay, the People's Republic of China, Romania, Spain (Barcelona), and Uruguay. New charts are added for four countries where deaf individuals or associations of the deaf have proposed them: Israel, Italy, West Germany (BRD), and Yugoslavia. Modifications in four charts have been made, based on information not available when the first edition was printed: France, Japan, Portugal, and the Republic of the Philippines.

I hope that this enlarged manual will be of further value to deaf and hearing individuals in communication with each other, and to scientific researchers in the fields of linguistics and anthropology investigating the diversity of sign languages in deaf communities around the world.

Appendix A contains some early manual alphabets from Austria, Germany, Hungary, and Switzerland. Because of strict oral education programs imposed in many areas of Europe, it is possible that earlier manual alphabets have disappeared completely from use. Those shown were lost for many decades until they were found again recently, and were made available to me for use in the second edition. Unfortunately, these alphabet charts do not come with definite information about sources or dates. Perhaps they can be traced in the near future through intensive research in national libraries or schools for the deaf in Europe.

Above all, I wish to acknowledge the many helpful suggestions that have enabled me to correct errors that have appeared in the first edition. Future comments and suggestions bringing to my attention typographical or drawing errors are more than welcomed.

SJC

INTRODUCTION

The main purposes for publishing various hand alphabet charts from other countries in this book are: 1) Deaf people from all over the world are beginning to travel to many countries and attend international affairs for the deaf, including the World Summer and Winter Games for the Deaf, and Congresses of the World Federation of the Deaf. They wish to communicate with their deaf fellows in the most convenient method by using a manual alphabet to specify certain words, names, or places. 2) This book may be of great assistance to those in various countries who would like to develop their own hand alphabets, to educate small deaf children for better communication. For instance, the Hebrew (Israel) and Persian (Iran) hand alphabet charts were made in the early 1970s after their creators had studied various charts from other nations. 3) The hand charts will be of great benefit to linguists for their studies of handshapes and other related matters.

Deaf-blind hand alphabet charts are included in this book. These may help readers become familiar with better methods to communicate with deaf-blind people, and help interested people to organize better educational and job programs for the deaf-blind.

The origin of the use of the hand alphabet, also called *dactylology,* is not known, although it had been practiced for many centuries before the Middle Ages. Very early, monks had employed the manual alphabet to communicate with each other without violating their strict vows of silence. Strangely, it was not applied for communication with the deaf.

Claiming that the Spanish people were the first to use the one-hand alphabet in teaching the deaf, several manuscripts and books document that the learned Benedictine monk named Pedro Ponce de Leon (1520-1584) was the very first instructor of the deaf around the middle of the 16th century, although there was no known manuscript or book describing a hand alphabet for the deaf (Bender 1970: 39-42; Werner 1932). A Franciscan monk, Fray Melchor de Yebra (1526-1586) was the first to write a book, *Libro llamado Refugium infirmorum* . . ., which describes and illustrates an actual hand alphabet for the particular use of deaf-mutes. It was not published until seven years after his death (Habig 1936: 287-292; Werner 1932:244). It is a rare work written at the end of the 16th century. (See the illustrations below.) There are 22 letters which are expressed by 21 signs since Y is the same as Z. Later, in 1620, in Madrid, Juan Pablo Bonet (1579-1629?) published the first known book for the teachers of the deaf, the earliest treatise on teaching the deaf to speak and write; it contains illustrations of the

Spanish hand alphabet (Bender 1970: 42-45; Farrar 1923: 9-14; Werner 1932). See Bonet's Spanish Hand Alphabet below, which closely resembles Yebra's illustrations of the hand alphabet.

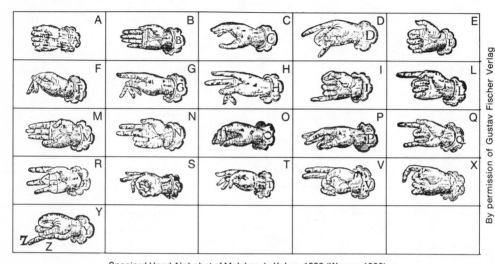

Spaniard Hand Alphabet of Melchor de Yebra, 1593 (Werner 1932)

Around the middle of the 18th century the Spanish manual alphabet was introduced into France by Jacob Rodriguez Pereire (1715-1780), who, it is claimed, was probably the first teacher of the deaf in France. Born at Berlanga in Spanish Estremadura, he belonged to a family of Spanish Jews who were expelled by persecution to Portugal and then to Bordeaux, in southern France, where they settled in 1741. Pereire had a deaf sister whom he had become interested in teaching. Seeking for a method of instructing the deaf, he probably received books from a friend in Spain, as early as 1734, and studied them. Possibly, one of them revealed to him the manual alphabet by Bonet. Later he started to instruct other deaf pupils. In 1749 he presented one of his outstanding deaf students before the French Academy of Sciences in Paris. Appointed by the Academy, a commission studied the value and results of Pereire's teaching method and especially commented on the important use of the manual alphabet. As a result, Pereire's achievements were recognized. The most distinctive feature of Pereire's method was the use of Spanish hand alphabet which he claimed to have expanded and augmented to conform to French orthography and pronunciation (Bender 1970:73-77; Farrar 1923:32-37; Lane 1976:171-172). But we have almost no information about the earliest uses of manual alphabets in France.

In 1760 the Abbé Charles-Michel de l'Epée (1712-1789) unexpectedly met two deaf twin sisters in Paris and became interested in them. He then decided to instruct them. He

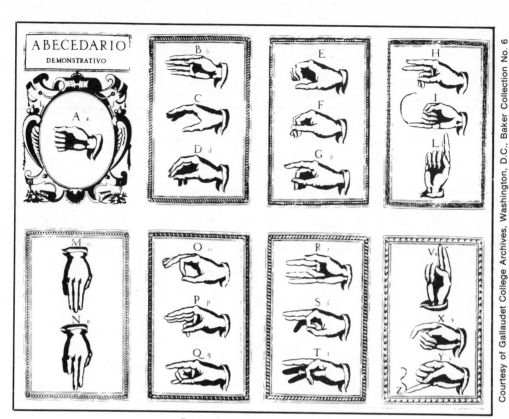

Bonet's Spanish Hand Alphabet, 1620

had known a two-handed alphabet since his childhood (Farrar 1923:40; Green 1861:12). Subsequently, he founded the first French public school for the deaf in Paris, regardless of social conditions. Some documents state that de l'Epée was acquainted with the teaching system employed by Pereire and used the manual alphabet in instruction (Farrar 1923:44), although he had never met Pereire nor any of his pupils (Green 1861:12). However, another document states that an admirer who had witnessed a public instruction, sold to de l'Epeé a Spanish book that contained a beautiful illustration of the manual alphabet of Bonet (Bender 1970:80; Farrar 1923:42-47).

After the death of the Abbé de l'Epée, Roche-Ambroise Sicard (1742-1822) became the director of the school in Paris. He continued the use of the one-handed alphabet, accompanied with methodical signs. An alphabet very similar to de l'Epée's was then brought to the United States by the young American Thomas Hopkins Gallaudet (1787-1851) who came to Paris in 1815 to acquire the art of teaching the deaf for his country. With French signs and the modified "Spanish" hand alphabet, Gallaudet returned to the United States in 1816, accompanied by Laurent Clerc (1785-1869), the gifted deaf French teacher. The following year, on April 15, 1817, the Hartford School for the Deaf was founded. Thus, the French manual alphabet with several modifications became the *American* hand alphabet.

Meanwhile, the French manual alphabet from Paris was introduced into different countries in Europe between 1779 and 1846 (von der Lieth 1967:63), with various modifications according to their respective linguistic orthographies. Other manual alphabets (for example, Austria, Denmark, Italy, Russia) have some clear similarities to the French alphabet, but they may have developed independently of the French traditions. We simply do not have enough historical information yet in this area.

The two-handed manual alphabet has been widely used in Great Britain since the seventeenth century. There is no record to reveal who the inventor of this system was, but it was published in a book, *Digiti Lingua*, by an anonymous author in London in 1698 (see page 26). The handshapes for vowels are very close to those of the British two-handed alphabet today. Most of the handshapes for consonants are also very close.

Two-handed alphabets similar to the British one were or are still in use in a number of countries. But in recent years there has been a trend to adopt a one-handed alphabet as an international standard, beginning with the Fourth Congress of the World Federation of the Deaf in Stockholm, Sweden in 1963. The alphabet adopted there is shown on page 87 as the International Hand Alphabet. Its varieties, and similarities and differences between it and the manual alphabet of the U.S.A., are discussed on page 76.

I would like to point out something interesting about the letter "T" in several hand charts, which is seemingly controversial. For instance, the American "T" is not used in France, Spain or other countries, because it is considered an extremely obscene sign in these countries, but it is a "good luck" sign in some South American countries. Therefore, the "T" from the Swedish chart was adopted in the international hand alphabet in order to lessen unfortunate connotations.

Any information or comments from readers regarding these or additional hand alphabet charts would be greatly appreciated.

Simon J. Carmel
1981

ACKNOWLEDGEMENTS

I wish to express my gratitude to the following people and organizations who were kind enough to send the hand alphabet charts, help me to obtain them, or discuss the subject of hand alphabet charts. I have listened to their suggestions, and benefited from their encouragement:

Reuben Altizer
Lloyd Anderson
Yerker Andersson
Chaim Apter
Raul Arbelaez
Carl A. Argila
Ritva Bergmann
Padmaja V. Bhide
Serena Bianchi
Nils Björö
Saliha Bousselham
Steven Chough
Henri Compere
William C. Dacanay
David L. de Lorenzo
Liz Elias
Ruth Feniger
Christy Foran
Andrew Foster
Marcial Godoy
Dr. Reinhart Graf
Corrine Hilton
António João de Jesus
Carolyn Jones
Friedrich-Wilhelm Jürgens
Akira Kiyota
Beat Kleeb
John W. Krpan
Gary Lensbower
Chin-heng Lim
Willard J. Madsen
Lidia Maldonado Garza de Rios
Czesław Małyszesyk
Harry Markowicz
Terttu and Carl-Eric Martola
Tom McLaren
Jean-Marie Michalon
Gheorghe Miclea

Padre Eugenio Oates
Noel Ostacchini
Frances M. Parsons
Armand Pelletier
Branimir Petani
Daniel Pokorny
Jean Claude Poulain
Maryam Rostami
Francesco Rubino
Julia Samii
Thorbjørn Sanders
Eli Savanick
Rick Schoenberg
George L. Schroeder
Maria Schwendenwein
Dorothy E. Shaw
Leonard Siger
Ann Silver
Salah M. Soliman
Knud Sondergaard
Theodore Staroyiannis
William C. Stokoe, Jr.
Mrs. Baron Sutadisastra
Jose M^a. Segimon Valenti
Rafael Edo. Valverde E.
Madan M. Vasishta
Edw. Verheesen
Lars von der Lieth
Dragoljub Vukotic
Gunilla Wågstrom
Gustav A. Weininger
Lee Chul Whan
Marshall Wick
Charles Yeager
John Tsu Chih Yeh
Hailu Yesuneh
Magda Zimet

Associacao Portuguesa de Surdos (Portuguese Association of the Deaf)
Association of the Deaf in Israel
Felag Heyrnalausra (Icelandic Association of the Deaf)
Gallaudet College/International Center on Deafness

Especially to Robert F. Panara for his *Foreword*.

My thanks to all other individuals and organizations (too numerous to mention) who in one way or another were of assistance to the author in preparing the present work.

I am especially indebted to the following:

The American School for the Deaf Museum, West Hartford, Connecticut, for their courtesy in reproducing the early American manual alphabet chart.

The Association of the Deaf in Israel for permission to reproduce the Hebrew hand alphabet.

Danske Døves Landsforbund for permission to reproduce the Danish hand alphabet chart.

The Encyclopedia Judaica and Keter Publishing House Jerusalem, Ltd., publishers of the *Encyclopedia Judaica,* for permission to reproduce the Hebrew manual alphabet on page 1420 and some important parts of the article, "Alphabet, Manual (Deaf)" on pages 744-745 of *Encyclopedia Judaica* (1971).

Gallaudet College Archives/Gallaudet College Library, Gallaudet College, Washington, D.C. 20002, for the use of several of the references and also for their courtesy in reproducing several old hand alphabet charts.

Alfredo Palau Garcia, the illustrator, for permission to reproduce the drawings of the Barcelona (Spanish) hand alphabet.

Gustav Fischer Verlag for permission to reproduce the 1593 Spaniard Hand Alphabet of Melchor de Yebra, from *Geschichte des Taubstummenproblems bis ins 17. Jahrhundert* by Hans Werner (1932).

Rosamund Hirschman, copyright owner, for permission to reproduce the Amharic alphabet in *Manual of Foreign Languages* (1952) by Georg F. von Ostermann on pages 353-354 for the use of the Ethiopian hand alphabet chart.

Friedrich-Wilhelm Jürgens for permission to reproduce the German (BRD) hand alphabet chart.

The National Center for Deaf-Blind Youths and Adults, New Hyde Park, New York, for permission to print three manual charts for deaf-blind people.

Norges Døveforbund for permission to reproduce the Norwegian hand alphabet chart.

The Royal National Institute for the Deaf, 105 Gower Street, London, for permission to reproduce the illustrations of the manual charts from *Conversation with the Deaf.*

Savez Gluvih Yugoslavie for permission to reproduce the Yugoslavian hand alphabet charts.

Bogdan Szczepankowski for permission to reproduce two old Polish hand alphabets on pages 6-7 of *Jezyk Migowy. Czesc II: Daktylografia* (1974).

Lars von der Lieth for his courtesy in reproducing the oldest Danish hand alphabet chart.

Youguang Zhou of People's Republic of China for permission to reproduce his article, "The Chinese finger alphabet and the Chinese finger syllabary", and the different hand charts.

Finally, I want to thank Lloyd Anderson and William C. Stokoe, Jr. for their comments and criticisms on this edition and also William R. Bozman and Joan N. Radner for their meticulous proofreading.

June, 1975
August, 1981

Simon J. Carmel
Rockville, Maryland, U.S.A.

HAND ALPHABET CHARTS

The Argentine hand alphabet chart designer—Simplicio

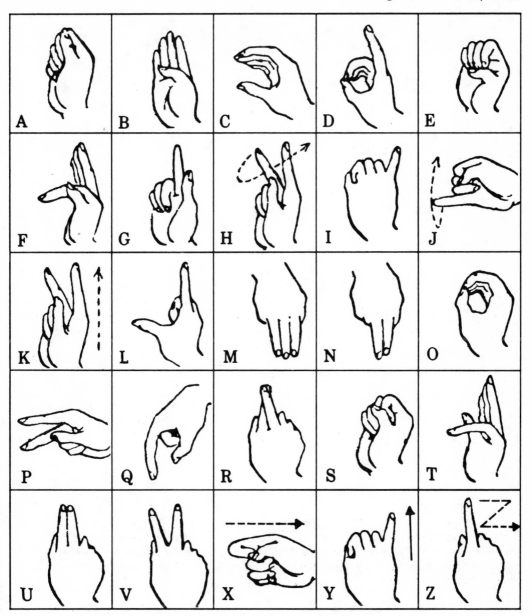

In the early years the British two-handed alphabet system was used in most states in Australia, except in Perth which had the American one-handed alphabet for several years. The latter was then replaced by the two-handed method in order to follow all the other states.

Later the Irish priests and sisters came to Australia and opened one convent school for boys and one for girls in N. South Wales. Deaf Catholics used the Irish one-handed alphabet while deaf Protestants used the two-handed. However, after a "professor" from England arrived there advocating oralism, the government through the department of education in all states accepted the method of oralism, and every deaf school including the Catholic convents abolished manualism for about fifteen years. In the early 1970's the Australian Federation of Teachers of the Deaf proposed to reinstate manualism, due to the poor standard of education results of the deaf pupils. They have at present adopted the combined method—lipreading and manualism.

A	B	C	D	E
F	G	H	I	J
K	L	M	N	O
P	Q	R	S	T
U	V	W	X	Y
Z				

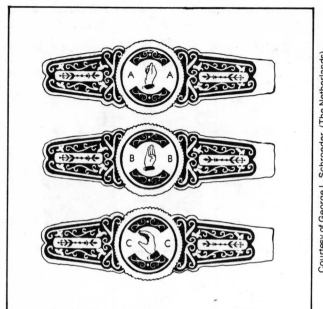

In the 1950s there was a very popular fad of collecting cigar bands in continental Europe. In Antwerp the late A. V. Peetersen, president of a Belgian club for the deaf, "Anverdos", learned that a hearing club, "Sibaver", was selling the cigar bands to hearing individuals with individual letters of the British two-handed alphabet. From this idea he started to print cigar bands with individual letters of the Belgian hand alphabet in 1958. See the illustrations above.

Between the 1950s and 1970s the associations of the deaf in Belgium and the Netherlands sold such cigar bands to raise funds in support of deaf organizations in their respective countries.

BELGIUM
Belgian Hand Alphabet

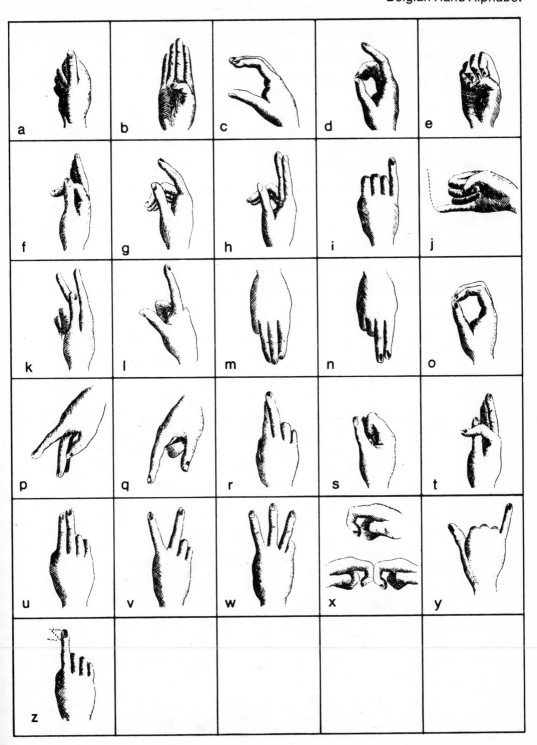

The manual alphabet used in Brazil is the alphabet invented by the famous French priest Abbé de l'Épée. No one knows exactly when it was introduced to the deaf of Brazil, but it was believed that it was in 1857 when a French teacher of the deaf helped the Brazilian Emperor Dom Pedro II found the first school for the deaf in Rio de Janeiro.

The Brazilian hand alphabet is most similar to the hand alphabet of Argentina.

Some special characteristics of the Brazilian letters and handshapes are:

> C is the regular C like the C of cat.
>
> Ç is a special Brazilian C that has a cedilla under it (mark like a comma) that indicates the sound of SS as in miss.
>
> G is made in the vertical position.
>
> H begins like U; turn the hand to the left and open the index and middle fingers slightly.
>
> K is raised slightly.
>
> X is moved inward slightly, with palm down.
>
> Y is moved forward slightly, breaking the wrist to the front.
>
> * Accents used on certain words are traced by the tip of the right index finger.

The chart below was published in 1875 by Flausino Jose da Gamma in Rio de Janeiro, Brazil.

6

A	B	C	Ç	D
E	F	G	H₁	H₂
I	J	K	L	M
N	O	P	Q	R
S	T	U	V	W
X	Y	Z		*Accents

A
B
C
D
E
F
G
H
I
J
K
L
M
N
Ñ
O
P
Q
R
S
T
U
V
W
X
Y
Z

COSTA RICA
Costa Rican Hand Alphabet

A	B	C	CH	D
E	F	G	H	I
J	K	L	LL	M
N	Ñ	O	P	Q
R	S	T	U	V
W	X	Y	Z	

FINGERSPROG ELLER HAANDALPHABET

til Brug i det Kongelige Inſtitut for Dövſtumme i Kiöbenhavn

Courtesy of Lars von der Lieth (Copenhagen, Denmark)

This is the earliest Danish manual alphabet, first used in 1807 when Peter Atke Castberg (1779-1823) founded the Royal Institute for the Deaf and Mute in Copenhagen.

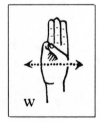

The printed letter "W" is not normally used in Danish words, but it is sometimes needed for proper names of persons or cities and foreign borrowed words.

"W" is like "V" except for an added movement.

12

A	B	C	D	E
F	G	H	I	J
K	L	M	N	O
P	Q	R	S	T
U	V	X	Y	Z
Æ	Ø	Å		

Please note that the Egyptian hand alphabet is read from right to left.

j 5 ج	th 4 ث	t 3 ت	b 2 ب	a 1 آ
r 10 ر	dh(ð) 9 ذ	d 8 د	kh(ẖ) 7 خ	ḥ 6 ح
ḍ 15 ض	sh(s) 14 ص	sh(š) 13 ش	s 12 س	z 11 ز
f 20 ف	gh(ɣ) 19 غ	(ʿ) 18 ع	ẓ 17 ظ	ṭ 16 ط
n 25 ن	m 24 م	l 23 ل	k 22 ك	q 21 ق
	y 28 ى	w 27 و	h 26 ه	

15

The Ethiopian hand alphabet was developed in 1975 by three deaf men (Minnasie Abera, Teklehaimanot Derso, and Hailu Yesuneh). The Ministry of Education in Ethiopia adopted it in 1976 for instructional purposes in schools for the deaf.

Ethiopic or Amharic is a Semitic language and a very ancient written language in Africa. As a syllabic language, Amharic has an alphabet consisting of more than 251 characters or letters, each representing a syllable. These consist of 2 base vowel characters and 31 base consonantal characters; each character has 7 variations or shapes.

For example, the Ethiopian consonant letters automatically include a vowel. To indicate six modified forms of the base letters (see opposite page), movements are added to the hand shapes to show the direction of the arrows, as below:

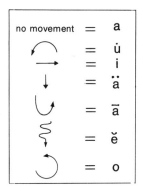

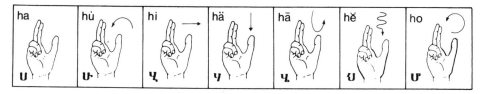

The American hand alphabet and hand numbers are also taught in Ethiopia.

The Ethiopian hand alphabet chart designer—Alemseged Araya

h **ሀ**	l **ለ**	ḥ **ሐ**	m **መ**	s **ሠ**
r **ረ**	s **ሰ**	sh **ሸ**	q **ቀ**	b **በ**
t **ተ**	ch(č) **ጠ**	ḫ **ጎ**	n **ነ**	ñ **ኘ**
(ʾ) **አ**	k **ከ**	kʰ **ኸ**	w **ወ**	(ʿ) **ዐ**
z **ዘ**	zh(ž) **ዠ**	y **የ**	d **ደ**	j(ǧ) **ጀ**
g **ገ**	t **ጠ**	ch(č) **ጨ**	p **ጰ**	ts **ጸ**
	ts **ፀ**	f **ፈ**	p **ፐ**	

17

For a long time, Finland used the Swedish hand alphabet. The old Finnish chart above makes this clear. Finland was once ruled by Sweden, although the offical spoken languages of Finland are Finnish and Swedish today.

After the Congress of the World Federation of the Deaf in 1963, Finnish deaf people, like the Norwegians, adopted the international hand alphabet system.

A B C D E
F G H I J
K L M N O
P Q R S T
U V W X Y
Z Å Ä Ö

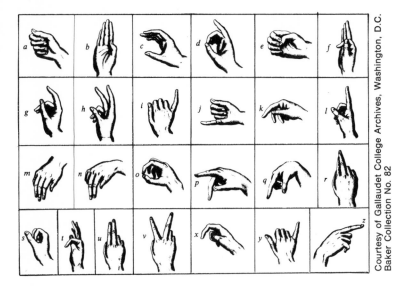

The chart above is probably one of the earliest French hand alphabet charts, published in Roche-Ambroise Sicard's *Cours d'instruction d'un sourd-muet de naissance* (1800).

In some areas of France, deaf people sometimes use *horizontal* variants of the letters M and N, as illustrated below, instead of the *vertical* variants (see the opposite page). The horizontal variants are more comfortable hand positions for fluent conversation.

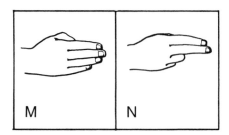

FRANCE

French Hand Alphabet

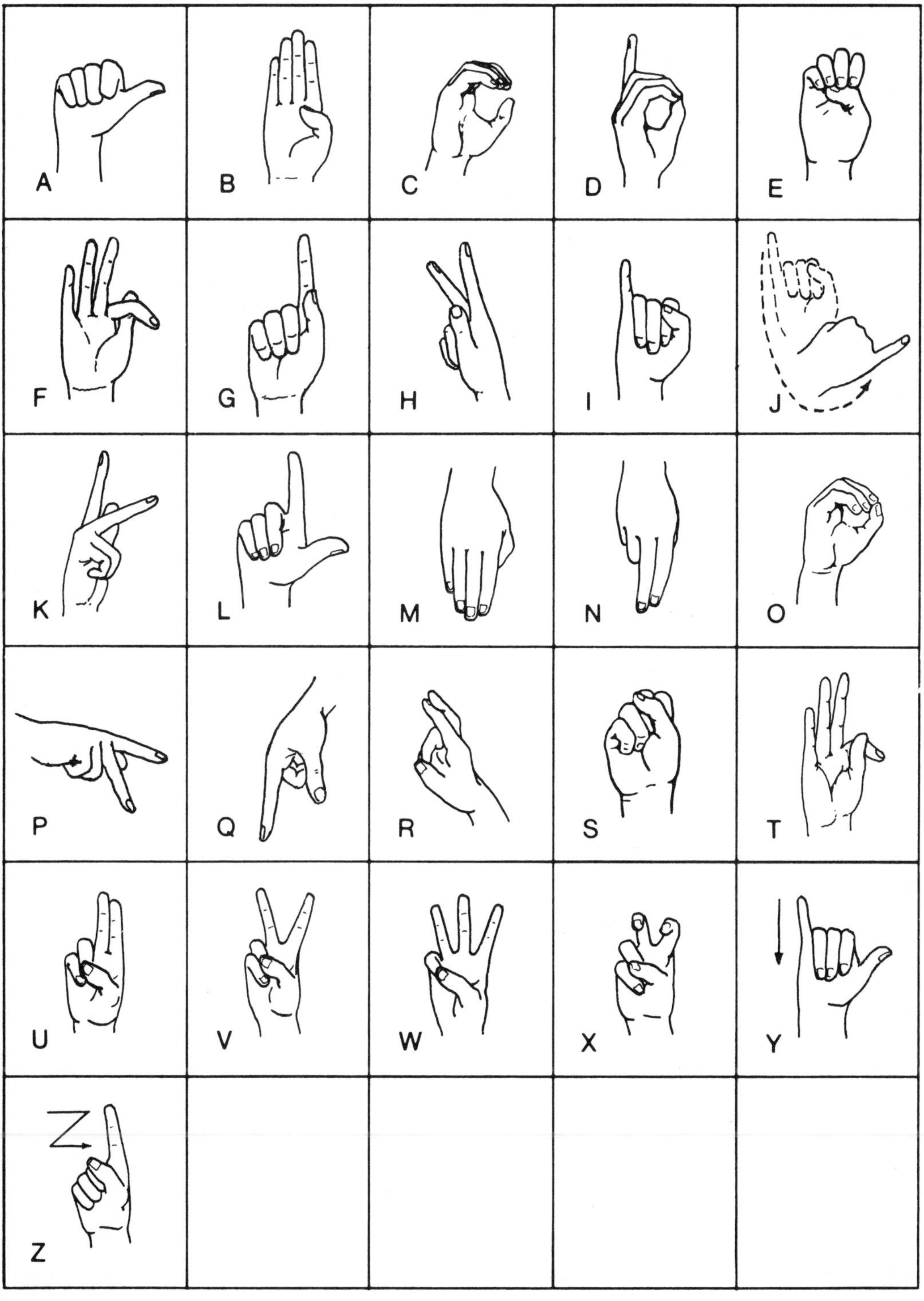

We have records of old manual alphabets in Germany, Switzerland, Austria, and Hungary (see Appendix A). These seem to be no longer in use, and were probably suppressed after the purely oral educational methods became dominant (Congress of Milan, 1880).

In 1956 Peter Rijntjes was introduced to the use of fingerspelling during his enrollment at the training center for future teachers of the deaf, in Euskirchen, near Bonn. For almost 20 years, Rijntjes taught classes for mentally retarded and multi-handicapped deaf pupils by means of writing, speech and also—occasionally—fingerspelling. However, intensive use of fingerspelling was not begun until the end of the 1960s, first by Fritz Geisperger, a teacher at the Straubing school for the deaf in southern Germany. Geisperger was influenced by his visit to Gallaudet College, in Washington, D.C. Reinhart Graf (1968) also used and published a manual alphabet.

Somewhat later Friedrich-Wilhelm Jürgens introduced fingerspelling in the Hildesheim school in northern Germany. Jürgens was influenced by the successes of fingerspelling methods in Leipzig (East Germany). Geisperger and Jürgens used the hand alphabet for the brighter pupils, and did not intend it especially for the mentally retarded or multi-handicapped.

The obvious successes of the fingerspelling methods have led to their spread in Germany. Young deaf students are pushing their use, and today there is at least one teacher at every school for the deaf who uses fingerspelling regularly. A television program for deaf audiences uses fingerspelling for names of people.

The manual alphabet adopted by Geisperger and others is like the alphabet used in the United States of America. Certain additional letters and combinations of letters have been needed, namely Ä, Ö, Ü, CH, SCH, ß (=SS). The three vowel letters were at first spelled by adding a motion (as in some historically older alphabets of Germany and Scandinavia). Later (according to Jürgens) the double motions were felt to be disruptive in fast fingerspelling, and so instead special hand *shapes* were adopted, distinguishing Ä, Ö, Ü from A, O, U. This way of indicating these vowel letters can also be seen in some older German manual alphabets. The handshape for SCH was borrowed by Jürgens from the East German fingerspelling. The handshape for CH was invented by one of his students.

In Austria the current German manual alphabet (opposite page) has occasionally been published in *Österreichische Gehörlosen-Zeitung* (Austrian Newspaper for the Deaf). Also, the same alphabet system was first adopted in the German-speaking area of Switzerland in 1981.

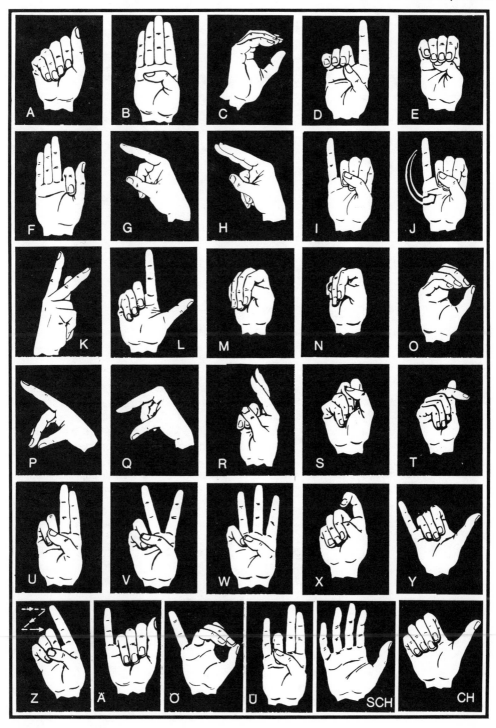

In East Germany (DDR), teachers tried using the Soviet program for early education of deaf children, which emphasized fingerspelling. The DDR was, in the early 1960s, the only country in central Europe where fingerspelling was officially attempted in Kindergartens. Russian fingerspelling was found to be very successful. The 1965, a group of teachers at the school for the deaf in Leipzig adopted the standard international hand alphabet with certain additional handshapes for the letter combinations SCH, CH, and ß (=SS).   The vowel letters Ä, Ö, and Ü were shown with an additional movement to distinguish them from A, O, and U (see opposite page), but sometimes a special hooking of the fingers was used to indicate Ü, as illustrated below:

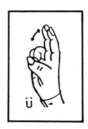

A	B	C	D	E
F	G	H	I	J
K	L	M	N	O
P	Q	R	S	T
U	V	W	X	Y
Z	Sch	Ch	β	

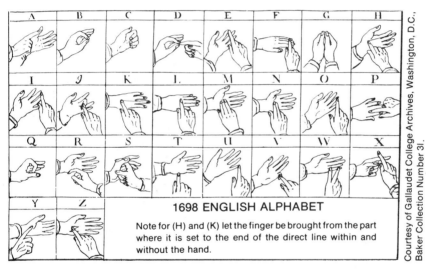

1698 ENGLISH ALPHABET

Note for (H) and (K) let the finger be brought from the part where it is set to the end of the direct line within and without the hand.

The chart above is probably the oldest British chart, from *Digiti Lingua*, London, 1698

The British two-handed alphabet (see opposite page) is widely used in Australia, England, India, New Zealand, Scotland, South Africa and other British Commonwealth nations.

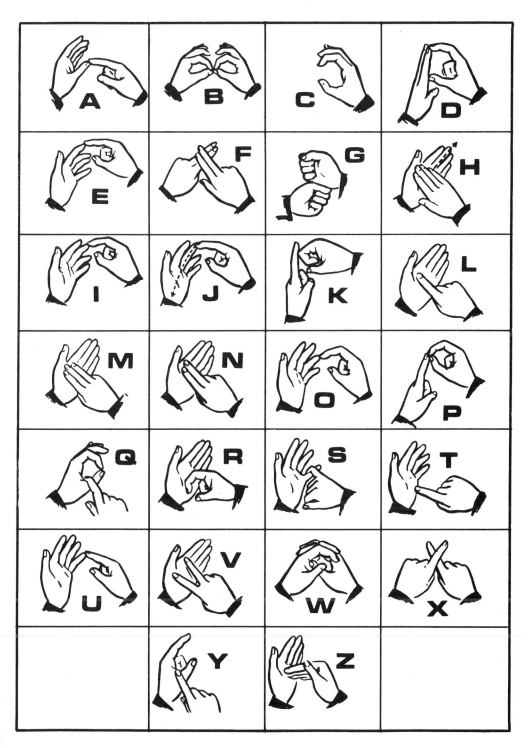

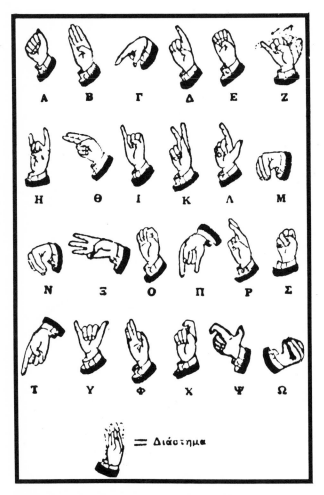

The chart above is the old Greek alphabet.
The new alphabet was revised in April 1975.

The Greek hand alphabet chart designer—Paul P. Munch

A	B	G	D
A	**B**	**Γ**	**Δ**

E	Z	I	TH
E	**Z**	**H**	**Θ**

I	K	L	M
I	**K**	**Λ**	**M**

N	X, KS	O	P
N	**Ξ**	**O**	**Π**

R	S	T	I
P	**Σ**	**T**	**Y**

F	CH	PS	O
Φ	**X**	**Ψ**	**Ω**

The Chinese language uses thousands of ideographic characters.
It has no alphabet.

But some Asian countries have adopted a fingerspelling alphabet.
They have a distinctive form of the letter "T" unlike most forms of "T"
used in Europe (but like Irish "T").

(These Asian alphabets have been provided by students at Gallaudet
College, in Washington, D.C., from these countries.)

HONG KONG, MALAYSIA, SINGAPORE, TAIWAN
Hand Alphabet

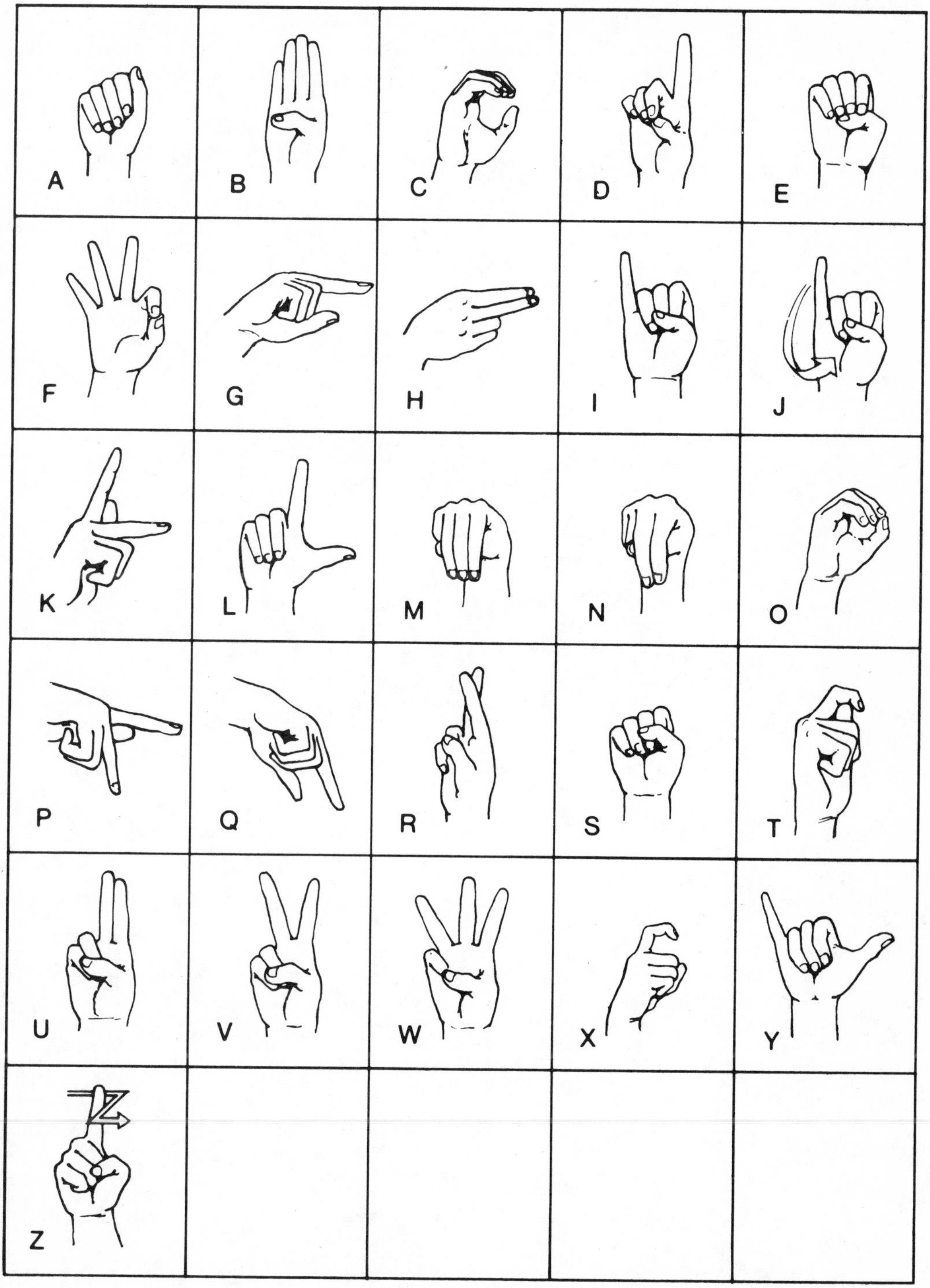

A	Á	B	C	D
Ð	E,É	F	G	H
I,Í	J	K	L	M
N	O,Ó	P	R	S
T	U,Ú	V	W	X
Y,Ý	Z	th Þ	Æ	Ö

Deaf people in India who know English have generally used a type of two-handed alphabet, historically related to the alphabet of Great Britain. Around Bombay, a small number of people use the manual alphabet of the U.S.A., which was brought there by Frances M. Parsons of the U.S.A. in 1974. But the two-handed alphabet is more accepted in India (for instance, see chart below). Deaf people who do not use English do not generally use any fingerspelling.

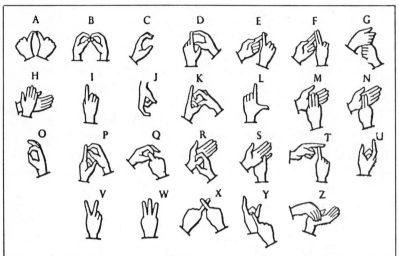

INDIA DEAF SOCIETY/Bombay - 1961

In 1976, a new manual alphabet (see the opposite page) was devised by Ms. Padmaja V. Bhide, representing the letters of the alphabet systems used in writing vernacular languages of India. Ms. Bhide was a teacher in the Stephen High School for the Deaf and Aphasic, in Bombay. She was assisted by three deaf people (Ramesh and Anil Phadke, two brothers, and Milind Adkar).

The Devnagri alphabet is used in several different forms for Hindi, Marathi, Gujarati, and other languages of India. In the manual alphabet given here, there are 36 handshapes for consonant letters and 12 handshapes for vowels and diphthong combinations. The vowels may be represented by separate letters and hand shapes (the first chart below).

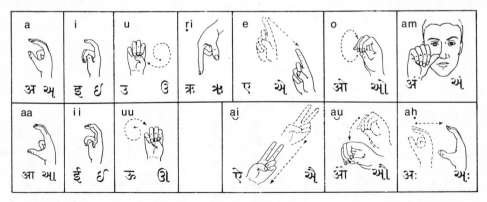

Note on the opposite page that the Hindi (& Marathi) written letter is shown on the *left* bottom; the Gujarati letter on the *right* bottom; and the standard English transcription on the *top*.

la. ळ	kṣa क्ष	jña ज्ञ	tra त्र	
	śa श	sha(ṣa) ष	sa स	ha ह
	ya य	ra र	la ल	va व
		ṅa ङ	na न	ma म
gha घ	jha झ	dha ढ	dha ध	bha भ
ga ग	ja ज	ḍa. ड	da द	ba ब
kha ख	chha छ	tha. ठ	tha थ	pha फ
ka क	cha च	ṭa. ट	ta त	pa प

Indonesian deaf people use a two-handed alphabet which is clearly related to the British and other two-handed alphabets of Europe. (Compare the letters B,C,D,G,K,M,N,P,Q,X, and Y with the British.)

However, in 1979 the Asian variety of the international manual alphabet was introduced for the first time in Indonesia. This differs from the European variety of the international manual alphabet principally in the letter "T" (shown below). This Asian alphabet is used also in Hong Kong, Malaysia, Singapore, and Taiwan.

A	B	C	D	E
F	G	H	I	J
K	L	M	N	O
P	Q	R	S	T
U	V	W	X	Y
Z				

Please note that the Persian (Iranian) hand alphabet is read from right to left.

s ⁶ ث	t ⁵ ت	p ⁴ پ	b ³ ب	a o e ā ² ا	ā ¹ آ
z ¹² ذ	d ¹¹ د	h ¹⁰ خ	h ⁹ ح	ch ⁸ چ	j ⁷ ج
s ¹⁸ ص	sh ¹⁷ ش	s ¹⁶ س	zh ¹⁵ ژ	z ¹⁴ ز	r ¹³ ر
f ²⁴ ف	gh ²³ غ	(') ²² ع	z ²¹ ظ	t ²⁰ ط	z ¹⁹ ض
n ³⁰ ن	m ²⁹ م	l ²⁸ ل	g ²⁷ گ	k ²⁶ ک	q ²⁵ ق
			y ³³ ی	h ³² ه	v ³¹ و

39

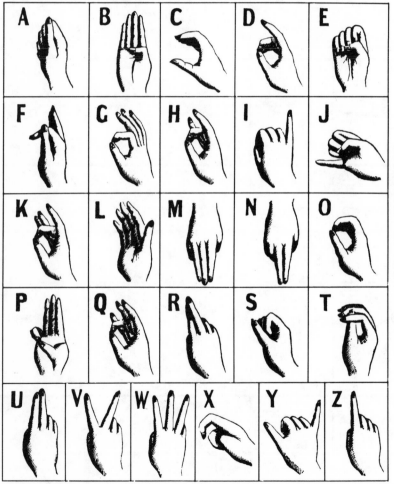

The Irish hand alphabet chart above was published in the first annual report of *Catholic Institution for the Deaf* in May, 1847.

Courtesy of Christy Foran (Dublin, Ireland)

IRELAND

Irish Hand Alphabet

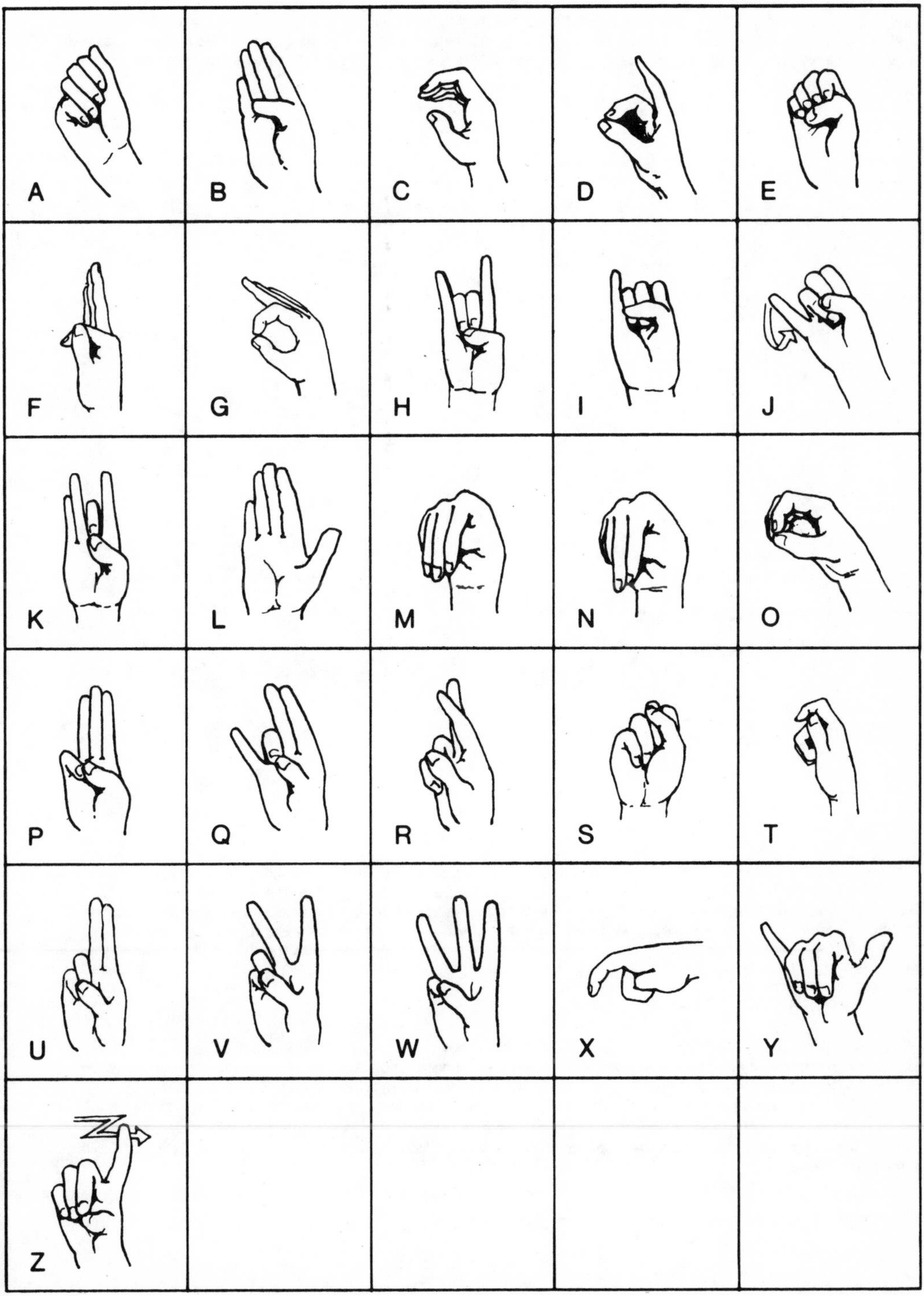

Three different manual alphabets have been proposed for Hebrew in recent times. The three designs have emphasized somewhat different principles. The two manual alphabets on this page took as their basic principle that the handshape should resemble the form of the printed letter so far as possible. The left alphabet was designed by Jonathan Shunary in 1968. The right alphabet was designed by Simon J. Carmel after extensive study and comparison of various manual alphabets of the world. It was published in the first edition of this book in 1975. In each of these two alphabets, a few of the letters are represented by handshapes of the International or American hand alphabets which represent similar sounds rather than letter forms (thus L, M, N, in Shunary's alphabet).

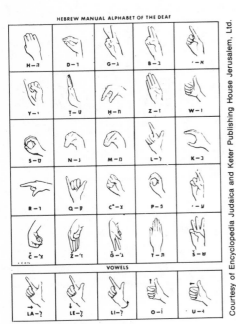

Shunary (1968)

Carmel (1975)

Courtesy of Encyclopedia Judaica and Keter Publishing House Jerusalem, Ltd.

The Hebrew alphabet chart designer—Ann Silver

The opposite page shows the new official Israeli hand alphabet developed in 1976 by Israel Sela, a hearing assistant director of the Association of the Deaf in Israel, with Hava Savir, a deaf teacher at Niv School for the Deaf in Tel Aviv. Since many manual alphabets in countries using the Latin written alphabet are similar to each other, and the International Hand Alphabet and the manual alphabet of the U.S.A. in particular are very close, they decided to use the same handshapes for similar *sound* values, disregarding the visual shape of the written letters. This gave them 16 letters: A,B,G,D,H,Z,I,C,L,M,N,S,P,K,R,T. Eight Hebrew letters (ב ו ח ט כ פ שׂ שׁ) required new handshape choices.

The vowelings of Hebrew writing are also represented differently by the three proposed alphabets. Shunary used different movements of the hand. For example, 1) Every consonant followed by an *a* vowel can be expressed by moving the palm being used to the right. 2) *e* vowels are expressed by moving the palm being used downward. 3) *i* vowels are expressed by a slight twist of the palm being used. 4) *o* vowels are expressed by pointing the thumb up. 5) The *u* vowel is expressed by pointing the thumb to the left and moving it in that direction.

Carmel based the hand shapes on the visual form of the written Hebrew voweling "points", and Sela and Savir have done the same.

Please note that the Hebrew hand alphabet is read from right to left.

The Israeli manual alphabet chart designer—Meir Noah ⟶

h **6**	d **5**	g **4**	v **3**	b **2**	ʾa (aleph) **1**
ה	ד	ג	ב	ב	א
k **12**	y **11**	ṭ **10**	kh(ḥ) **9**	z **8**	v,w **7**
פ	י	ט	ח	ז	ו
n **18**	m (final) **17**	m **16**	l **15**	kh(ḥ)(final) **14**	kh(ḥ) **13**
נ	ם	מ	ל	ך	כ
f (final) **24**	f **23**	p **22**	ʿa (ayin) **21**	s **20**	n (final) **19**
ף	פ	פ	ע	ס	ן
s **30**	sh(š) **29**	r **28**	ḳ(q) **27**	ts(ṣ)(final) **26**	ts(ṣ) **25**
ש	שׁ	ר	ק	ץ	צ
e **34**	a **33**	ā **32**		ALPHABET → VOWELS ← ← VOWELS	t **31**
··	־	־			ת
ə (sheva) **40**	o,ô **39**	û **38**	u **37**	i **36**	ɛ **35**
׃	־ , וֹ	וּ	···	··	··

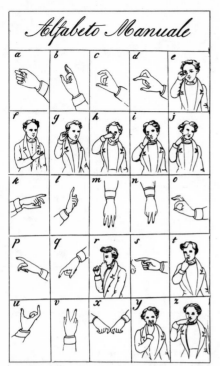

The chart above is the earliest Italian alphabet, probably in the early 1850's. (Sources: Cullingworth [1902], p. 15; Holycross [1913], p. 31)

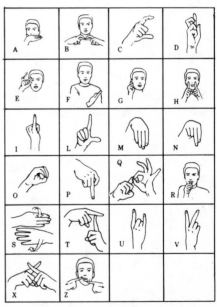

The manual alphabet above is somewhat obsolete, but deaf or hearing people are still using it in some areas in Italy. Some Italian-Americans also use it.

The Italian deaf people are now using to some extent the official Italian hand alphabet (opposite page).

The Italian hand alphabet chart designer — A. Perocchio

A	B	C	D	E
F	G	H	I	J
K	L	M	N	O
P	Q	R	S	T
U	V	W	X	Y
Z				

The Japanese language does not have an alphabet. It was originally written in Chinese characters borrowed from China during the 5th century. Around the 9th century a system of syllabic notation was developed to have 47 basic syllables consisting of five vowels: A-I-U-E-O, one single consonant and 41 consonant-vowel syllables. This is called the *kana* system which has two forms: *hiragana* that is the cursive (written with the letters joined together), and *katakana* that is the squared form. The latter is for use in children's books, telegrams and in transliterating foreign names and words. In the charts here, the Japanese system given is the *hiragana*.

The chart below represents two kinds of diacritical marks that are added to some of the *kana* to produce voiced sounds (sonants) as follows:

["] is designed for a voiced sound. For example, ka → ga, ki → gi, sa → za, shi → ji, ta → da, tsu → zu. The hand position moves sidewards.

[°] is designed for a p-sound. For example, ha → pa, hi → pi, fu → pu, he → pe, ho → po. The hand position moves upwards.

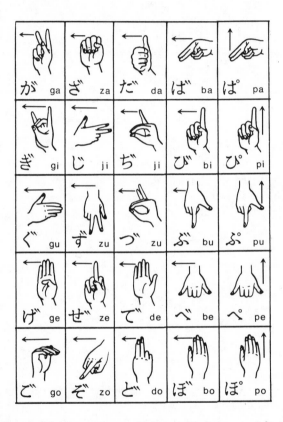

が ga	ざ za	だ da	ば ba	ぱ pa
ぎ gi	じ ji	ぢ ji	び bi	ぴ pi
ぐ gu	ず zu	づ zu	ぶ bu	ぷ pu
げ ge	ぜ ze	で de	べ be	ぺ pe
ご go	ぞ zo	ど do	ぼ bo	ぽ po

When つ *tsu* is inserted before a *kana* starting with k, p, s, or t, that consonant is doubled. For example, また *mata* becomes まった *matta* (not matsuta). The hand position moves backwards (see illustration below).

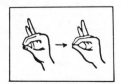

JAPAN
Japanese Hand Alphabet

n ん				
wa わ				(wo) を
ra ら	ri り	ru る	re れ	ro ろ
ya や		yu ゆ		yo よ
ma ま	mi み	mu む	me め	mo も
ha は	hi ひ	fu ふ	he へ	ho ほ
na な	ni に	nu ぬ	ne ね	no の
ta た	chi ち	tsu つ	te て	to と
sa さ	shi し	su す	se せ	so そ
ka か	ki き	ku く	ke け	ko こ
a あ	i い	u う	e え	o お

47

KOREA
Korean Hand Alphabet

k,g ㄱ	n ㄴ	t,d ㄷ	l,r ㄹ	m ㅁ	p,b ㅂ
s, hs ㅅ	o ㅇ	j,ch ㅈ	ch ㅊ	k ㅋ	t ㅌ
p ㅍ	h ㅎ	z, sh ㅆ	a ㅏ	ya ㅑ	
u ㅓ	yu ㅕ	o ㅗ	yo ㅛ	oo ㅜ	yoo ㅠ
eu ㅡ	ee, i ㅣ	ea ㅐ	yea ㅒ	e ㅔ	ye ㅖ
wo ㅚ	woe ㅚ	wee ㅟ			

49

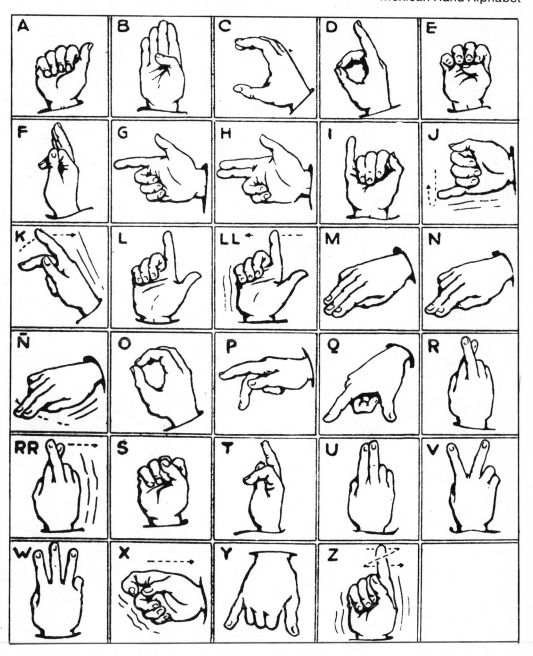

The Dutch hand alphabet is closest to the Belgian one (with the exception of the letter of "W") and both of these are close to the French.

Fingerspelling was virtually abolished in all schools for the deaf in the Netherlands, except in some northern parts of the country. Deaf people still use it outside school and at job or social gatherings for the deaf.

THE NETHERLANDS

Dutch Hand Alphabet

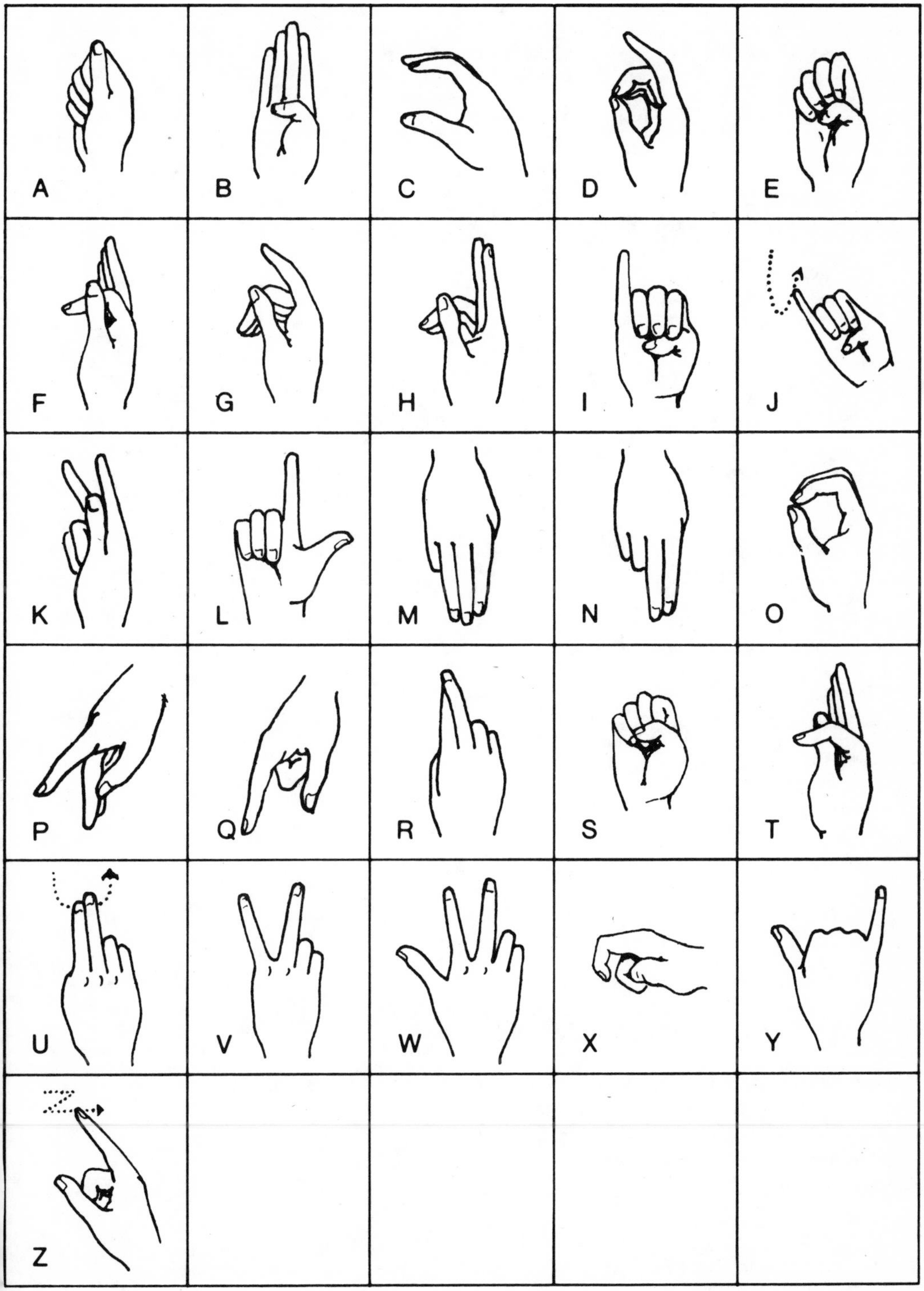

This is an old hand alphabet chart for Denmark and Norway.

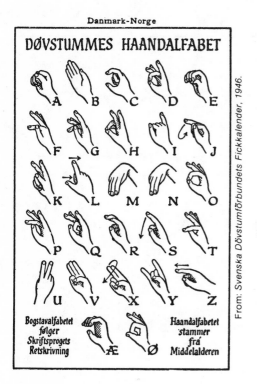

DØVSTUMMES HAANDALFABET

A B C D E
F G H I J
K L M N O
P Q R S T
U V X Y Z

Bogstavalfabetet
følger
Skriftsprogets
Retskrivning
Æ Ø

Haandalfabetet
stammer
fra
Middelalderen

From: Svenska Dövstumförbundets Fickkalender, 1946.

The Norwegian hand alphabet is not like the Swedish hand alphabet, in spite of Sweden's being Norway's neighbor, but is more similar to the Danish one because Norway once belonged to Denmark before the Napoleonic War. This explains why Norway used the Danish system.

Norway officially adopted the international hand alphabet system after the Congress of the World Federation of the Deaf in 1963.

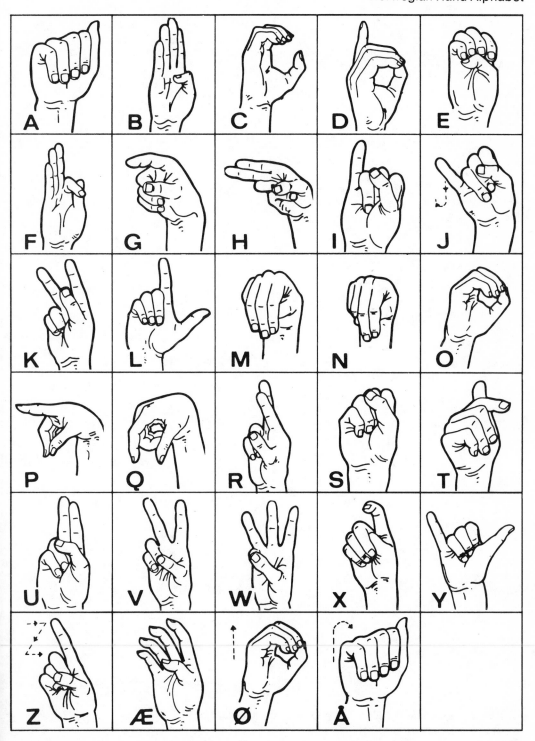

The Paraguayan manual alphabet seems to be a variant of the U.S. alphabet, but with an additional letter for Ñ.

A	B	C	D	E
F	G	H	I	J
K	L	M	N	Ñ
O	P	Q	R	S
T	U	V	W	X
Y	Z			

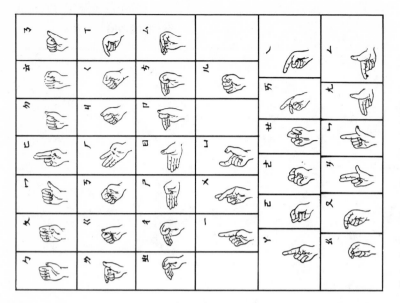

Figure 2. Later Zhuyin Zimu manuals (1930)

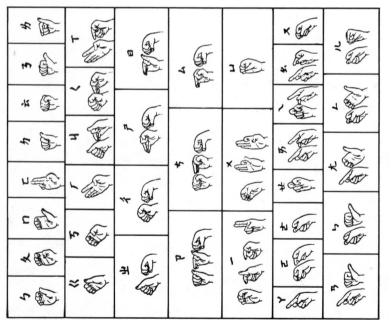

Figure 1. Early Zhuyin Zimu manuals (1918)

The Chinese language does not have any alphabet at all but has thousands of ideographic characters.

For more details about the Chinese hand charts, see the article in Appendix B on page 111.

PEOPLE'S REPUBLIC OF CHINA

Chinese Hand Alphabet

Figure 3. Pinyan finger alphabet (1963)

A	B	C	D	E	F
G	H	I	J	K	L
M	N	O	P	Q	R
S	T	U	V	W	X
Y	Z	ZH	CH	SH	NG

an	ang	in	ing	un
ong	ian	iang	uan	uang
ai	uai	ei	uei	ao
iao	ou	iou	ie	üe

59

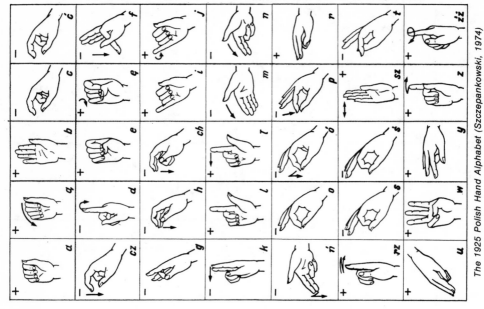

The 1925 Polish Hand Alphabet (Szczepankowski, 1974)

The 1817 Polish Hand Alphabet (Szczepankowski, 1974)

A	Ą	B	C	Ć	CH
CŻ	D	DZ	DŹ	DŻ	E
Ę	F	G	H	I	J
K	L	Ł	M	N	Ń
O	Ó	P	R	RZ	S
Ś	SZ	T	U	W	Y
Z	Ź	Ż			

▼ DRUGI ZNAK

DLA LITER:
Ć, DŹ, Ń, Ó, Ś, Ż

* Second sign for letters

61

In 1806 a Swedish government official named Pär Aron Borg came to see a play entitled, "Abbé de l'Epée or the Deaf and Dumb", at The Royal Theater in Stockholm, Sweden. This play was about the education of deaf children. Borg then became interested in teaching the deaf (Ahlner 1918:3-4). Subsequently he established the first Swedish school for the deaf outside Stockholm in 1809. Later Portugal heard of Borg's success, and invited him to establish a school for the deaf in Lisbon, Portugal in 1823.

For some unknown reasons he did not accept the French hand alphabet. It is often claimed that he invented the Swedish hand alphabet, but it may have existed before him. There is not yet enough evidence to decide this question. It is possible that he introduced the Swedish alphabet into Portugal when he went there. It is interesting to note that the present-day Portuguese alphabet has 18 handshapes which are similar to the Swedish ones.

A | B | C | D | E

F | G | H | I | J

K | L | M | N | O

P | Q | R | S | T

U | V | W | X | Y

Z

REPUBLIC OF THE PHILIPPINES
Philippine Hand Alphabet

A	Ă , Î	B	C	D
E	F	G	H	I
J	K	L	M	N
O	P	Q	R	S
Ş	T	Ţ	U	V
W	X	Y	Z	

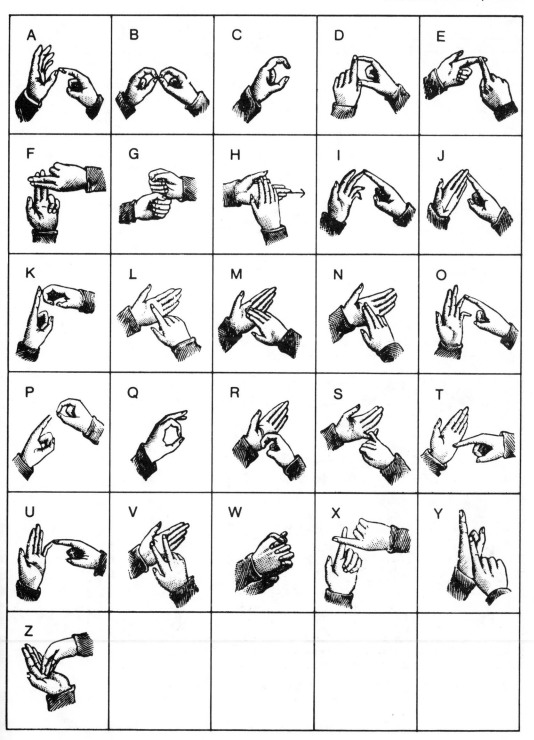

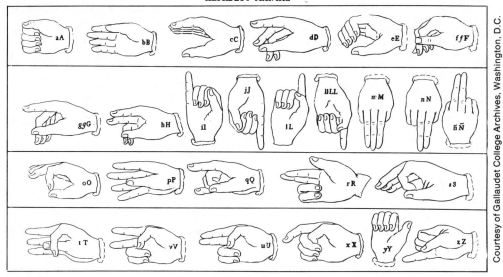

The chart above was published by Hervas in 1795.

The chart below based in Madrid, was published by Ballestreros and Villabrille in 1851.

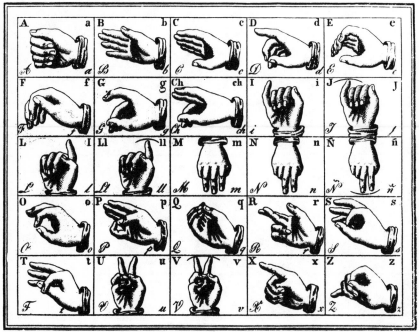

There are two slightly different variants of the Spanish hand alphabet (see the opposite page) in Madrid and Barcelona, as indicated.

The Barcelona hand alphabet chart designer - Alfredo Palau Garcia

SPAIN
Spanish Hand Alphabet

in Barcelona

D	I	N	R	W	
CH	H	M	Q	V	
C	G	L	P	U	Z
B	F	K	O	T	Y
A	E	J	Ñ	S	X

in Madrid and Barcelona

E	I	M	Q	U	Z
D	CH	LL	P	T	Y
C	H	L	O	S	X
B	G	K	Ñ	RR	W
A	F	J	N	R	V

This is an old hand alphabet chart for Sweden and Finland.

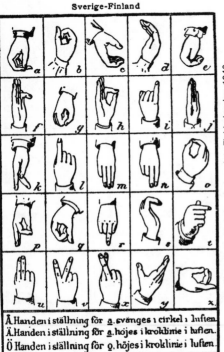

Sverige-Finland

Å.Handen i ställning för a. svänges i cirkel i luften.
Ä.Handen i ställning för a.höjes i kroklinie i luften.
Ö Handen i ställning för o.höjes i kroklinie i luften.

From: Svenska Dovstumforbundets Fickkalender, 1946

Please see the notes on page 62 (Portuguese hand alphabet).

A	B	C	D	E
F	G	H	I	J
K	L	M	N	O
P	Q	R	S	T
U	V	W	X	Y
Z	Å	Ä	Ö	

The Thai language is a tonal language. In the written language there are five different tones. It has 44 consonant *letters*. These consonant *letters* represent only 20 different consonant sounds, but each letter also indicates one of the three tones - High, Middle, and Low.

The Thai hand alphabet was based on the American one, using the American handshapes for Thai letters with the same sounds as much as possible. It uses two hands. The right hand is for the 44 consonants and 7 of the vowels. The left palm is for other vowels and four marks of tone. The index finger of the right hand has to point at the position required on the left palm. To mark a tone, point at the tip of one of the four fingers. Twenty-one (21) distinctive vowels are formed by these combinations.

(Source: Krairiksh, *Why Manual Language is Necessary for the Thai Deaf* [ca 1956])

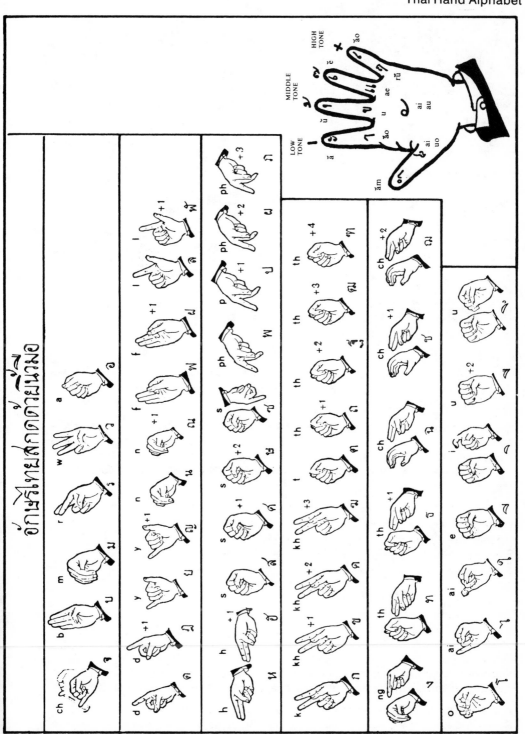

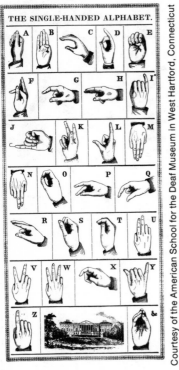

THE SINGLE-HANDED ALPHABET.

Courtesy of the American School for the Deaf Museum in West Hartford, Connecticut

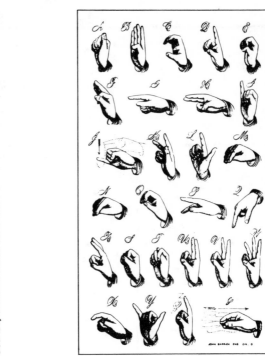

Courtesy of Gallaudet College Archives, Washington, D.C.

Dr. Thomas Hopkins Gallaudet and Laurent Clerc brought the French hand alphabet to the United States of America from Paris, France, in 1816 in order to start teaching the deaf children in Hartford, Connecticut.

The chart above to the left is one of the earliest American hand alphabet charts. It was published for the first time in L. Weld's *The 27th Report of the Directors of the American Asylum, at Hartford, for the Education and Instruction of the Deaf and Dumb* (1843). The chart on the right, with new drawings, first appeared in J. Williams' *The 65th Annual Report* (1881).

In various parts of the United States deaf people use variant handshapes for the letters of "G", "H", and "P". See illustrations below. Note that some deaf people use the letter "P" with the thumb near the tip of the middle finger while the letter "K" is used with the thumb placed between the forefinger and the middle finger.

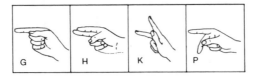

Today the American manual alphabet is widely used in many countries around the world, including Ghana, Ivory Coast, Jamaica, Liberia, Nigeria and Trinidad & Tobago.

In Canada deaf people are using the U.S. one-hand alphabet in many places, but the British two-handed alphabet is still being used in some areas of Eastern Canada.

76

UNITED STATES OF AMERICA

American Hand Alphabet

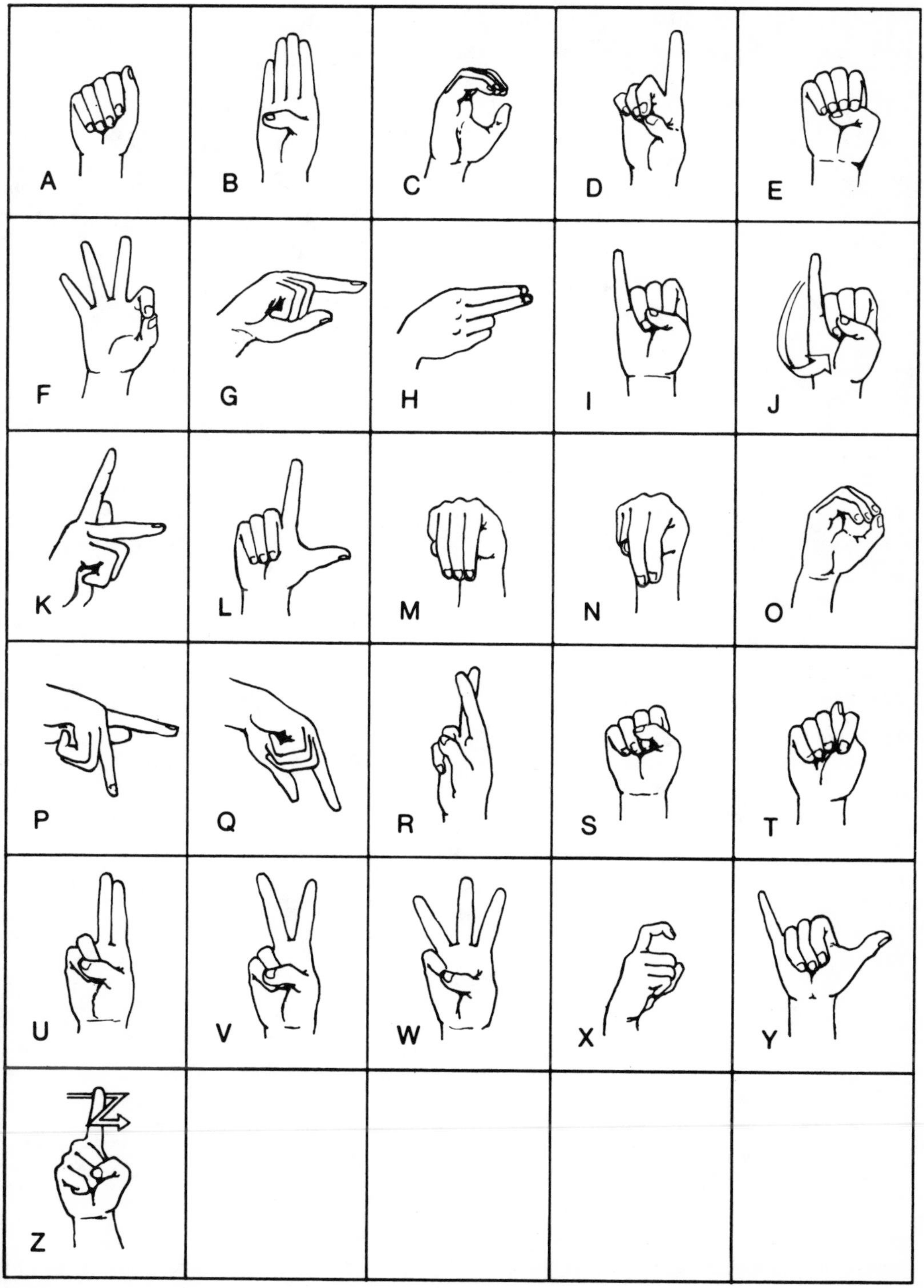

A	B	C	CH	D
E	F	G	H	I
J	K	L	LL	M
N	Ñ	O	P	Q
R	S	T	U	V
X	Y	Z		

The Russian hand alphabet is also used in Bulgaria.

Ъ =hard sign, used after a consonant to separate it from a vowel.
ь =soft sign, used after a consonant to soften it.

a	b	v	g	d	ye	zh
А	**Б**	**В**	**Г**	**Д**	**Е**	**Ж**

z	i	ĭ	k	l	m	n
З	**И**	**Й**	**К**	**Л**	**М**	**Н**

o	p	r	s	t	oo	f
О	**П**	**Р**	**С**	**Т**	**У**	**Ф**

kh	ts	ch	sh	shch	hard sign	i
Х	**Ц**	**Ч**	**Ш**	**Щ**	**Ъ**	**Ы**

soft sign	e	yu	ya			
Ь	**Э**	**Ю**	**Я**			

81

A	B	C	D	E
F	G	H	CH	I
J	K	L	LL	M
N	Ñ	O	P	Q
R	S	T	U	V
W	X	Y	Z	

83

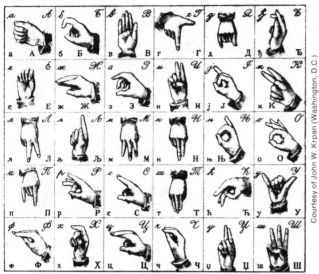

РУЧНА АЗБУКА ЗА ГЛУВОНЕМУ ДЕЦУ.

ПО ПРЕДАВАЊУ ЈОВАНА БОЉАРИЋА УЧИТЕЉА – БЕОГРАД, 1894 ГОД.

The earliest Yugoslavian manual alphabet (1894)

The two official modern manual alphabets (opposite page) have been introduced recently. They use the same handshapes but they are shown in different alphabetical orders, according to the orders of the Latin and Cyrillic alphabets. In general, in the western part of Yugoslavia the language is written with Latin script, and in the eastern part the Cyrillic script is used.

84

Cyrillic alphabet

Latin alphabet

The International Hand Alphabet shown here was adopted at the Fourth Congress of the World Federation of the Deaf (WFD) in Stockholm, Sweden, in 1963. The handshapes are similar to those of the standard hand alphabet in the United States of America, and also to several other one-handed alphabets of Europe.

Differences are most obvious in forms of the letter "T". The handshape used for "T" in the U.S.A. is regarded as an obscene gesture in France, parts of South America, Italy, Spain, Romania, and many other countries. In Europe there are two handshapes used widely for "T". The one shown here is used mainly in northern Europe. Another handshape with the weaker fingers opened (see for example France) is used mainly in southern Europe, and in parts of South America. A third handshape is used in certain nations of Asia (see for example Hong Kong). We might thus speak of "dialects" of an International Hand Alphabet, slight differences which do not make serious problems for communication among deaf people.

INTERNATIONAL HAND ALPHABET CHART

HAND ALPHABET CHARTS
FOR THE DEAF-BLIND

Communication with a deaf-blind person who knows the one-handed alphabet can be quite rapid. The finger positions are formed within his cupped hand. Certain letter formations are closely related, and it often speeds memorizing if they are learned in the following groups and in the order given: (A C E O S T) (D G H I J L X Z) (K P) (M N Q) (B F R U V W Y).

AMERICAN ONE-HANDED MANUAL ALPHABET

For the Deaf-Blind

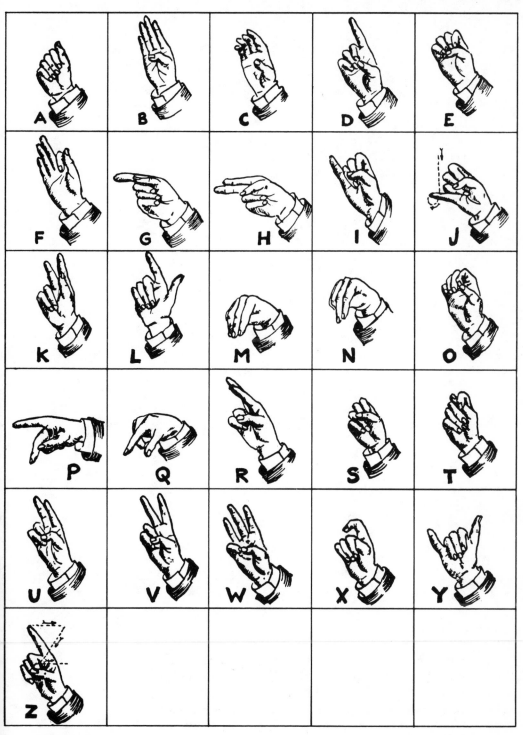

This is the British hand alphabet for the deaf-blind, which was improved by Mr. Edward Evans, C.B.E, M.P., Vice-Chairman of the National Institute for the Deaf in London, England.

The chart represents that the speaker or interpreter firmly presses his or her right hand against the left hand of the deaf-blind person.

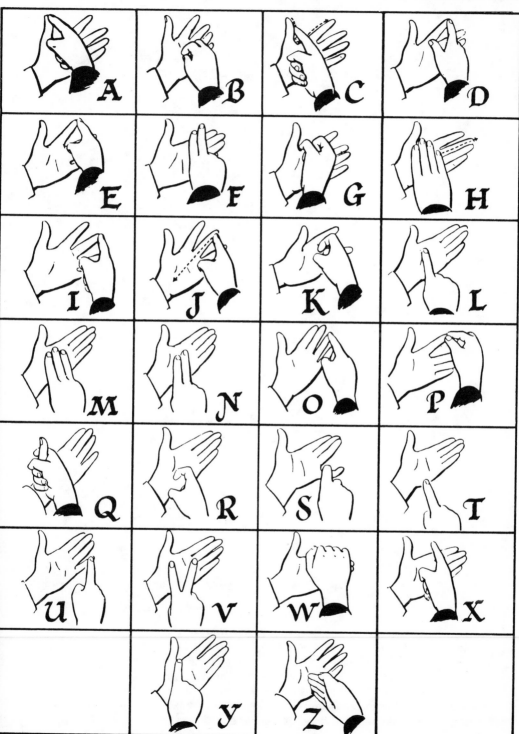

Anyone who can print simple block letters can make immediate use of the international standard manual alphabet in communicating with most deaf-blind persons. Lines, arrows, and numbers indicate proper direction, sequence, and number of strokes. Print only in palm area. Do not try to connect letters. Complete one, pause, then complete the next on the same palm area. Pause longer at the end of a word.

INTERNATIONAL STANDARD MANUAL ALPHABET

For the Deaf-Blind

A 2 STROKES	**B** 2 STROKES	**C** 1 STROKE	**D** 2 STROKES	**E** 4 STROKES
F 3 STROKES	**G** 1 STROKE	**H** 3 STROKES	**I** 1 STROKE	**J** 1 STROKE
K 2 STROKES	**L** 1 STROKE	**M** 1 STROKE	**N** 1 STROKE	**O** 1 STROKE
P 2 STROKES	**Q** 2 STROKES	**R** 2 STROKES	**S** 1 STROKE	**T** 2 STROKES
U 1 STROKE	**V** 1 STROKE	**W** 1 STROKE	**X** 2 STROKES	**Y** 2 STROKES
Z 1 STROKE				

THE LORM ALPHABET

The Lorm Alphabet, developed in Europe in 1881, has been for many years the most popular system for communicating with the deaf-blind in Germany, Austria, and Holland. It is also used in the United States.

In using the Lorm Alphabet, the "reader's" hand may be touched on the palm or on the back, according to preference.

The symbols used in the chart are as follows:

A SINGLE DOT—touch the spot indicated on the hand with the tip of one finger.

TWO OR MORE DOTS TOGETHER—touch the place indicated with the number of fingers shown by the number of dots.

A SINGLE ARROW—move the tip of one finger along the place and in the direction shown by the arrow; where the arrow is next to the hand rather than on it, the finger should move along the side of the hand rather than on the surface.

THREE PARALLEL ARROWS—move the whole flat of the hand along the reader's hand in the direction indicated.

TWO SHORT ARROWS POINTING TOWARD EACH OTHER AT THE FINGERTIPS— squeeze together the tips of the fingers indicated.

LORM ALPHABET
For the Deaf-Blind

A	B	C	D	E
F	G	H	I	J
K	L	M	N	O
P	Q	R (drum with fingertips)	S	T
U	V	W	X	Y
Z	YES	NO	WORD END	

A	B	C	D	E
F	G	H	I	J
K	L	M	N	O
P	Q	R	S	T
U	V	W	X	Y
Z	Æ	Ø	Å	

APPENDICES

APPENDIX A : Some Earlier Hand Alphabets in Europe

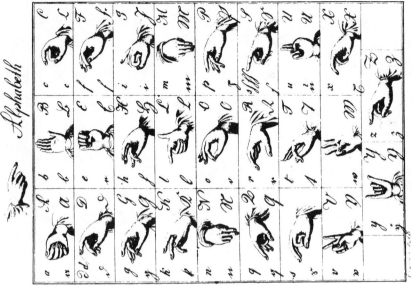

Courtesy of Gallaudet College Archives, Washington, D.C.
Baker Collection Number 147

Published by Anton Schwarzer (1828).

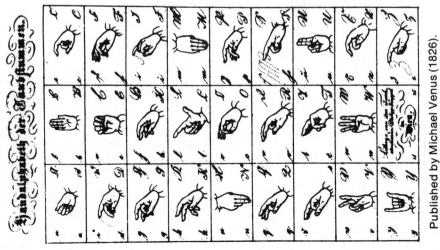

Courtesy of Gallaudet College Archives, Washington, D.C.
Baker Collection Number 134

Published by Michael Venus (1826).

The Austrian chart above was contributed by Dr. Maria Schwendenwein of Vienna, Austria. Its exact source and date are not known.

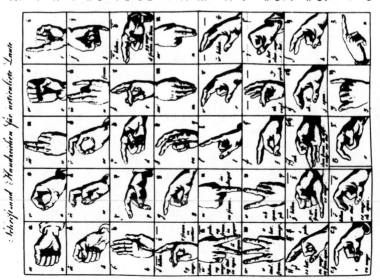

Old Austrian hand alphabet published by Franz H. Czech (1836).

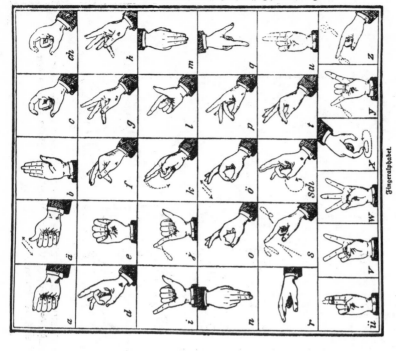

Published by G. Riemann in 1916.

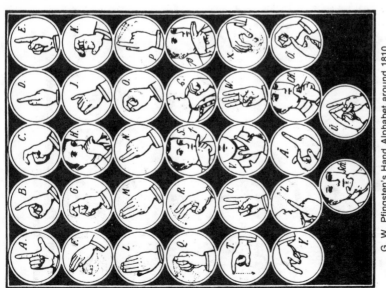

G. W. Pfingsten's Hand Alphabet around 1810

Used in Schleswig, in the northern part of West Germany, the Pfingsten chart (Emmerig 1927:62) has 32 hand signs, including signs for Ä, Ö, Ü, CH, ˙ SCH, ß, with partly static, and partly mobile positions. There are 29 one-handed signs, and 3 two-handed signs. Six of the one-handed signs are made on the face.

This German chart is reprinted from *The Abbé de l'Epée* by E. I. Holycross (1913:32), but its exact source and date are not known.

The Hungarian manual alphabet chart (opposite page) was contributed by Magda Zimet, a deaf woman from Budapest. No further information is available on its source or date.

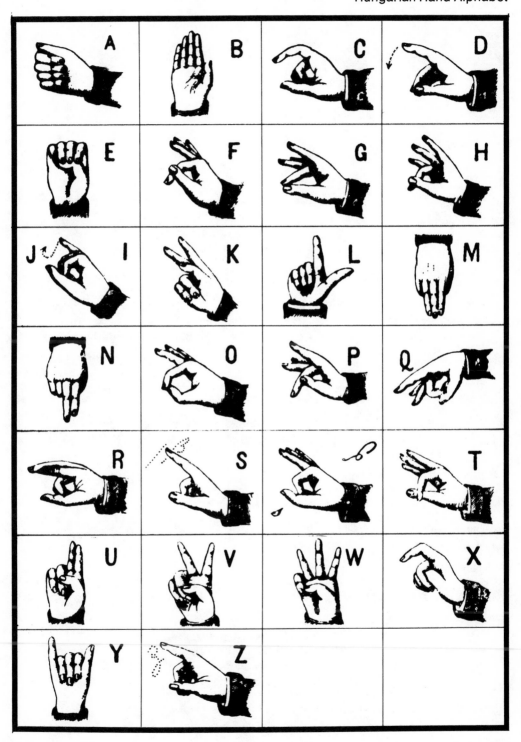

To date no special Swiss hand alphabet has appeared. This is due to the fact that, since the 18th century, Switzerland and some neighboring countries such as Austria and Germany have had the most strongly oral tradition of deaf education, following the philosophy of the German educator Samuel Heinicke.

However, today some Swiss deaf people are using the International Hand Alphabet. In addition, they are in process of deciding whether or not they will use the German hand signs for CH, SCH, and the umlaut as Ä, Ö, and Ü (see for example page 23).

In 1979 the old Swiss hand alphabet was contributed by Beat Kleeb of Uetikon am See, Switzerland. The drawing was made by the deaf artist Heinrich Bollier (1834-1897) in 1886 and dedicated to his school for the blind and deaf in Zürich.

It is interesting to note two important elements of the drawing: 1) The hand alphabet of Zürich closely resembles the old French manual alphabet (see example page 20), except for the handshape letter of "P", and 2) A man in the lower right corner works on a statue of Abbé de l'Epée, the founder of the first French public school for the deaf in Paris. Evidently, the French method of instructing deaf children was introduced in Switzerland in the 1820s (von der Lieth 1967:63).

The German poem is translated as follows:

To the Deaf-Mute:

To be sure, you know not the beautiful voice
which, kind and consoling, is your brother's by choice.
Mute stays the lip and closed is the ear,
but gaily you raise your glance to "hear"
what Earth and Sky impart to your mind,
what you in a loving eye can find!
That is the voice which speaks to you,
And what it says you know is true.

An die Taubstummen.

Wohl kennet Ihr die Stimme die schöne nicht,
Die freundlich und tröstend zum Bruder spricht,
Stumm bleibt die Lippe, verschlossen das Ohr,
Doch freudig hebt Ihr den Blick empor,
Was Erd und Himmel Euch still vertraut,
Was Ihr im liebenden Auge schaut,
Das ist die Stimme die zu Euch spricht,
Und Ihre Sprache, sie tauschet nicht.

Dem Blinden & Taubstummen-Institut in Zürich gewidmet von H. Bolber, ehm. Zögling.

APPENDIX B: The Chinese Finger Alphabet and the Chinese Finger Syllabary

by Youguang Zhou

I. The Chinese Finger Alphabet

About ninety years ago, an American missionary, Mrs. A. T. Mills, devised the first system of Chinese manual symbols and taught it in her school for the deaf at Cheefoo (Yantai) in China's Shandong Province. She used A. M. Bell's visible speech symbols to denote the sounds of Chinese characters, and Edmund Lyon's manuals to denote the speech symbols.

In 1918, the Chinese phonetic symbols in characters called Zhuyin Zimu were published. Lyon's manuals were then used to denote Zhuyin Zimu, as in Fig. 1, page 58.

Later, around 1930, the Zhuyin Zimu manuals were somewhat improved by a Shanghai school for the deaf, as in Fig. 2, page 58.

In 1958 the Chinese phonetic alphabet in Romanization called Hanyu Pinyin (or simply Pinyin) was officially adopted to replace Zhuyin Zimu. This led to a new Chinese Finger Alphabet, published in 1963, with 30 finger forms to represent the 26 Roman letters and the 4 digraphs (ZH, CH, SH, and NG) of Pinyin, see Fig. 3, page 59.

Compared with the former methods, this new Finger Alphabet is simpler and more practicable. The finger forms are designed according to four principles: (1) The *first* principle is to imitate the graphs of Roman letters. For instance, a complete circle represents the letter O, and a broken circle represents C. The letters B, D, E, F, H, K L, M, N, P, S, V, W, X, Y and Z are imitated less nicely. (2) The *second* principle is to borrow the sounds by acrophony from traditional Chinese finger forms. For instance, the traditional finger form "one" (yi) is used for I, "five" (wu) for U, "seven" (qi) for Q, "nine" (jiu) for J, "rabbit" (tur) for T. (3) The *third* principle is to borrow the meaning. For instance, thumb-up, meaning first or best, for letter A. The last or little finger represents NG, which always comes last in spelling Chinese syllables. (4) The *fourth* principle is variation. For instance, finger forms Z, C and S are slightly varied to become ZH, CH and SH. The rarely used diacritical marks (·· ^) are indicated by a slight shaking of the hand. The four tone marks (– ´ ˇ `) are "written in the air" only when necessary. All finger forms are made with one hand only, either right or left, but usually with the right hand.

II. The Chinese Finger Syllabary

During the 1950s, education of the deaf in China underwent a big reform by changing silent speech to sound speech. Formerly most pupils learned to "read" but not to speak, and now lipreading and pronunciation have become required training. Since the 1960s the Chinese Finger Alphabet and the Roman letters of Pinyin are used in almost every school for the deaf.

However, it has been found that the alphabetic finger forms have to move and shift incessantly. Chinese syllables are composed of 1-4 letters (or digraphs), and most Chinese words have one or two syllables. The finger forms are changing all the time from one to another, on the average three changes to make one syllable. It is not easy for the pupils to catch the syllables and words. As a result, there is a new method called Chinese Finger Syllabary developed to make it possible to see the syllabic finger forms clearly. The explanations are given as follows:

111

Every Chinese syllable (except those beginning with a vowel, like *an* "peaceful") can be divided into two parts, the initial and the final. Initials are consonants. Finals are vowels or vowels with endings. For instance, *ba* (eight) can be divided into *b* and *a*; *kai* (open) into *k* and *ai*, *tian* (heaven) into *t* and *ian*, etc. If the initials are represented by the right hand and the finals by the left hand, and both hands are raised up at the same time, syllables can be shown wholly and steadily.

The Chinese Finger Alphabet has already provided finger forms for initials (consonants) and simple finals (vowels). It needs only supplementary finger forms for the compound finals, and the Chinese Finger Syllabary will come into being.

This is done according to the five following principles. (1) By division of labor: with the left hand, the finger form Y (named *ya* in Pinyin) will stand for IA, W (named wa) for UA, R for ER, N for EN, and NG for ENG. (2) By change of direction to indicate nasal endings (-n, -ng) : the finger forms A, I, U, IA and UA pointing to the left stand for AN, IN, UN, IAN and UAN, and pointing to the right for ANG, ING, UNG(ONG), IANG and UANG, respectively. (3) By conditional combination: after J, Q and X, the finger forms ONG, UAN and UN become IONG, üAN and üN, respectively; after B, P, M and F, the finger form O becomes UO. (4) By special formation: the finger forms AI, EI, AO and OU (the so-called four open finals) are formed as shown in Fig. 4, page 59 . (5) By variations: the finger forms AI, EI and AO pointing to the right for UAI, UEI (UI) and IAO, respectively; E pointing upward for IE, and pointing forward for üE. These five principles make the method easier to remember.

The work of designing the Chinese Finger Syllabary began in 1974, and experimentation started in the following year. The designers are Prof. ZHOU Youguang and Mrs. SHEN Jiaying, both of whom are also co-designers of the Chinese Finger Alphabet. Mrs. Shen, a teacher, has undertaken the experimentation in her school, the Fourth School for the Deaf of Peking, with the cooperation of her fellow teachers. Years of practice have proved that the new method of the Chinese Finger Syllabary is a success, but it still remains for the government to accept it formally.

References

Xu, Jinwen (Zhou, Youguang), 1965. A primer to deaf-mutes and Lyon's manuals. *In* Essays on the Chinese Finger Alphabet. Peking: Wenzi Gaige Publishing House.

Shen, Jiaying, 1964. Developments in the Chinese Finger Alphabet. *Wenzi Gaige Monthly,* March issue.

Zhou, Youguang, 1964. Characteristics and usages of the Chinese finger alphabet. *Guangming Ribao Daily News.* March 4.

Hong, Xueli, 1965. Ways and methods of the reform of manual speech. *In* Essays on the Chinese Finger Alphabet. Peking: Wenzi Gaige Publishing House.

[Youguang Zhou, the author, is Research Fellow of the Committee for the Reform of Chinese Written Language and Professor at the Research Institute of Language and Writing, People's University of China.]

(This article is essentially the same as the original which appeared as "The Chinese Finger Alphabet and the Chinese Finger Syllabary", but it is abridged and there are a few editorial changes.)

BIBLIOGRAPHY

Abernathy, Edward R., 1959. An historical sketch of the manual alphabets. *American Annals of the Deaf* 104 (2) : 232-241.

Ahlner, Oscar G , ed., 1918. *Martrikel över svenska dövstumskolan: 1809—1918* (History of the Swedish Schools for the Deaf: 1809—1918). Lund, Sweden: Carl Bloms Boktryckeri. 505 pages.

Amin, Moh., *et al.*, eds., 1975. *Pedoman Praktis: Penyelenggaraan Skolah Luar Biasa: Bagien B - Tuna Rungu Wicara* (Practical Guidance for the Special Education Program: Section B - for the Deaf). Jakarta, Indonesia: Department of Education and Culture. 97 pages.

Anderson, Lloyd, 1976. Handshape changes in the history of fingerspelling. Unpublished manuscript. 33 pages.

_____, 1979. Sign language number systems and the numerical alphabet. *In* The Sciences of Deaf Signing. Børge Frøkjaer-Jensen, ed. Pp. 1-34. Copenhagen: Audiologopedic Research Group, Copenhagen University Amager.

_____, 1980. Origin of hand alphabets in older hand numerals. (This takes the place of parts of the preceding item.) Talk presented at the Hamburg International Congress on Education of the Deaf, and at the Linguistics Department, Copenhagen University Amager.

_____, forthcoming. *A History of Hand Alphabets and Hand Counting.*

Anonymous, 1698. *Digiti Lingua.* 30 pages.

Australian Catholic Schools for the Deaf, 1943. *How to Converse with the Deaf in Sign Language, As Used in the Australian Catholic Schools for the Deaf.*(Compiled by the Teachers of the Schools at Waratah and Castle Hill, New South Wales) Newcastle, Australia: Davies & Cannington Pty., Ltd., Printers. 132 pages.

Baker, Charlotte, and Dennis Cokely, 1980. *American Sign Language: A Teacher's Resource Text on Grammar and Culture.* Silver Spring, Maryland: T. J. Publishers, Inc. 469 pages.

Ballestreros, Juan Manuel and Francisco Fernandez Villabrille, 1851. *Revista de la ensenanza de los sordo-mudos y de los ciegos* (Review of Teaching of the Deaf-Mutes and the Blind). Madrid, Spain: Imprenta De Dicho Colegio. 427 pages.

Bender, Ruth E., 1970. *The Conquest of Deafness.* Revised edition. Cleveland, Ohio: The Press of Case Western Reserve University. 243 pages.

Bhide, Padmaja, 1977. *Finger-spelling for Indian Language.* Bombay, India: National Society for Equal Opportunity for the Handicapped. 16 pages.

Bonet, Juan Pablo, 1620. *Reduction de las letras y arte para enseñar à ablar los mudos.* (Simplification of the Letters of the Alphabet and Method of Teaching Deaf Mutes to Speak). Madrid: Abarca de Angulo. 334 pages.

Bravo, Ermida, Rafael Edo. Valverde, and Gloria Campos, 1979. *Hacia una neuva forma de comunicacion con el sourdo* (Toward a New Form of Communication with the Deaf). San Jose, Costa Rica: Ministerio de Educacion Publica. 184 pages.

Brooklyn. Industrial Home for the Blind, 1959. *Rehabilitation of Deaf-Blind Persons, Volume II, Communication: A Key to Service for Deaf-Blind Men and Women.* Brooklyn, New York: The Industrial Home for the Blind. 70 pages.

Cabiedas, Juan Luis Marroquin, 1975. *El lenguaje mimico* (The Sign Language). Madrid, Spain: Tall. gráficos de la Fed. Nac. de Soc. de Sordomudos de España. 76 pages.

Carmel, Simon J., 1975. *International Hand Alphabet Charts.* First edition. Rockville, Maryland: Studio Printing Inc. 96 pages.

Catholic Institution for the Deaf and Dumb, 1847. *Catholic Institution for the Deaf and Dumb. First Annual Report, May 1, 1847.* Dublin, Ireland: William Powell. 46 pages.

Cullingworth, William R., 1902. *A Brief Review of the Manual Alphabet of the Deaf.* Chicago: Wm. R. Cullingworth, Engraver and Publisher. 16 pages.

Czech, Franz Herrmann, 1836. *Versinnlichte Denk- und Sprachlehre, mit Anwendung auf die Religions- und Sittenlehre und auf des Leben* (Illustrated Thought and Language Doctrine, with Application to the Doctrine of Religion and Morals and to Life). Wien: Gedruckt und in Commission der Mechitaristen-Congregations-Buchhandlung. 444 pages.

Deschamps, Claude Francis (The Abbé), 1779. *Course élémentaire d'éducation des sourds et muets* (Elementary Course for Education of the Deaf and Mute). Paris: Debure. 362 pages.

Emmerig, Ernst, ed., 1927. *Bilderatlas zur Geschichte der Taubstummenbildung* (Picture Atlas of the History of Education of the Deaf-Mute). München, Germany: Taubstummendruckerei & Verlag Otto Maidl.

Ethiopian National Association of the Deaf, 1976. *Courage* Magazine. First edition. Addis Ababa, Ethiopia: Ethiopian National Association of the Deaf. Number 1, p. 18. July.

Farrar, Arnold, 1923. *Arnold on the Education of the Deaf. A Manual for Teachers.* Second edition. London: The National College of Teachers of the Deaf. 415 pages.

Finnish Association of the Deaf, 1973. *Viittomakielen kuvasanakirja* (Sign Language Picture Book). Helsinki, Finland: Finnish Association of the Deaf. 440 pages.

Fondelius, Elsa, 1971. *Teckenordbok* (Dictionary of the Signs). Borlange, Sweden: Sveriges Döves Riksförbund. 103 pages.

da Gama, Flausino José, 1875. *Iconographia dos signaes dos surdos-mudos* (Iconography of Signs for the Deaf-Mute). Rio de Janeiro, Brazil: Typographia Universal de E. & H. Laemmert. 79 pages.

Geilman, Iosif F., 1957. *Ruchnaia azbuka i rechevye zhesty glukhonemykh* (The Manual Alphabet and the Signs of the Deaf). Moscow: Vsesoiuznoe Kooperativnoe Izdatel'stvo. 596 pages.

Geisperger, Fritz, 1968. Das Fingeralphabet als Sprachmittel in Kindergarten (The finger alphabet as a means of communication in [the] kindergarten). *In* Früherziehung für hörgeschädigte Kinder. Sonderheft 1. Pp. 50-53. Kettwig, Germany: Hörgeschädigte Kinder.

Goodstadt, Rose Yin-Chee, 1972. *Speaking with Signs*. Hong Kong: Government Printer. 341 pages.

Graf, Reinhart, 1968. Handzeichensysteme und ihre Möglichkeiten für die Früherziehung (Hand sign systems and their possibilities for early education). *In* Früherziehung für hörgeschädigte Kinder. Sonderheft 1. Pp. 45-49. Kettwig, Germany: Hörgeschädigte Kinder.

Green, Francis, 1861. Extracts from the *Institution des Sourds et Muets* of the Abbé de l'Epée. Translated. *American Annals of the Deaf* 13 (1): 8-29.

Habig, Marion A., 1936. The first manual alphabet. *Catholic Educatonal Review* 34 (5): 286-292.

Hervas y Panduro, Lorenzo, 1795. *Escuela Española de Sordo-Mudos, o Arte Para Enseñarles a Escribir y Hablar el Idioma Español* (Spanish School for Deaf-Mutes or Art of Teaching them to Write and Speak the Spanish Language). Madrid: Fermin Villalpando. Volume I: 335 pages; Volume II: 376 pages.

Holycross, Edwin Isaac, 1913. *The Abbe de l'Epee: Founder of the Manual Instruction of the Deaf, and Other Early Teachers of the Deaf.* Columbus, Ohio: Edwin Isaac Holycross, Publisher. 72 pages.

Humphries, Tom, Carol Padden, and T. J. O'Rourke, 1980. *A Basic Course in American Sign Language*. Silver Spring, Maryland: T. J. Publishers. viii and 280 pages.

Japanese Association of the Deaf, 1973. *Watashi tachi no tebanashi* (Our Hand Talk). Tokyo, Japan: Japanese Association of the Deaf. Five volumes. 977 pages.

Jones, Harry, 1968. *Sign Language*. London, England: The English Universities Press Ltd. 180 pages.

Jónsdóttir, Thuridur, 1976. *Táknmál* (Icelandic Sign Language Book). Reykjavik, Iceland: Félagi heyrnarlausra og Foreldra-og styrktarfélagi heyrnardaufra (The Icelandic Deaf Organization and The Association of the Parents of Deaf Children). 186 pages.

Jussen, Heribert, and Michael Krüger, 1975. *Manuelle Kommunikationshilfen bei Gehörlosen: Das Fingeralphabet* (Manual Communication Aids Among Deaf People: The Finger Alphabet). Berlin-Charlottenburg, Germany: Carl Marhold Verlagsbuchhandlung. 171 pages.

Krairiksh, Kamala, ca 1956. *Why Manual Language is Necessary for the Thai Deaf.* 28 pages (Xerox copy of the manuscript can be purchased through Gallaudet College Library, Gallaudet College, Washington, D.C. 20002).

Krasnich, I. N., and Sokolyanskii, I. A., 1954. *Bukvar dlya shkol vzroslich gluchonemich* (School Primer for Deaf Adults). Second Edition. Moscow. 174 pages.

Lane, Harlan, 1976. *The Wild Boy of Aveyron.* Cambridge, Massachusetts: Harvard University Press. 401 pages.

Long, J. Schuyler, 1963. *The Sign Language: A Manual of Signs.* Reprint of second edition. Washington, D.C.: Gallaudet College. 222 pages.

Namir, Lila, Israel Sella, M. Rimor, and I. M. Schlesinger, 1977. *Dictionary of Sign Language of the Deaf in Israel.* Jerusalem, Israel: Hamakor Printing House Ltd. 221 pages.

Nicholas, O.P., Sister M., et al., 1979. *The Irish Sign Language.* Dublin, Ireland: The National Association of the Deaf. 120 pages.

Oates, C.SS.R., Eugênio, 1969. *Linguagem das mãos* (Language of Hands). Rio de Janeiro, Brazil: Gráfica Editora Livro S. A. 325 pages.

Oleron, Pierre, 1974. *Elements de repertoire du langage gestuel des sourds-muets* (Elements of the Repertory of Sign Language of the Deaf-Mutes). Paris, France: Centre National de la Recherche Scientifique. 174 pages.

O'Rourke, Terrence J., 1970. *A Basic Course in Manual Communication.* Silver Spring, Maryland: The National Association of the Deaf. 132 pages.

Orpen, Charles E. H., 1836. *Anecdotes and Annals of the Deaf and Dumb.* Second edition. London: Robert H. C. Tims. 626 pages.

Pelissier, P., 1856. *Iconographie des signes, avec des notes explicatives* (Iconography of Signs with Explanatory Notes). Paris: Paul Dupont. 46 pages.

Plum, Ole Munk, 1967. *Handbog i Tegnsprog* (The Sign Language Handbook). Copenhagen, Denmark: Danske Døves Landsforbund. 367 pages.

Plum, Ole Munk, et al., 1979. *Dansk-Tegn Ordbog* (The Danish Sign Language Dictionary). Copenhagen, Denmark: Danske Døves Landsforbund. 382 pages.

Prata, Maria Isabel, 1980. *Mãos que falam* (Hands That Talk). Lisboa, Portugal: Laboratório de Fonética da Faculdade de Letras/Universidade de Lisboa and Direccão Geral do Ensino Básico. 109 pages.

Rammel, Georg, 1974. *Die Gebärdensprache: Versuch einer Wesensanalyse* (Sign Language: Attempt at an Essential Analysis). Berlin-Charlottenburg, Germany: Carl Marhold Verlagsbuchhandlung. 132 pages.

Riemann, G., 1916. *Taubstumm und blind zugleich* (The Deaf-Mute and the Blind Together). Berlin: Schriftenvertriebsanstalt. 107 pages.

Rossellio, R. P. F. Cosma, 1579. *Thesaurus Artificiosae Memoriae.* Venice: 146 pages.

Roth, Professor Cecil, and Dr. Geoffrey Wigoder, eds., 1971. *Encyclopedia Judaica.* Jerusalem, Israel: Keter Publishing House Ltd.

Royal National Institute for the Deaf, 1968. *Conversation with the Deaf.* Chichester, Sussex, England: Chichester Press Ltd. Booklet Number 491, 8th Edition. 41 pages.

Rubino, Francesco, 1975. *Gestuno: International Sign Language of the Deaf.* Carlisle, England: The British Deaf Association. 254 pages.

Schwarzer, Anton, 1828. *Lehrmethode zum Unterrichte der Taubstummen in der Tonsprache für Lehrer* (Teaching Methods for Instruction of Deaf-Mutes in the Spoken Language). Often, Austria: Universitäts-Schriften/Carl Schaumburg. 519 pages.

Sela, Israel, 1977. Israeli fingerspelling (Hebrew text). *Sa'ad Bimonthly for Social Welfare* 21 (1): 44-46 (January).

Sicard, Roche-Ambroise, 1800. *Cours d'instruction d'un sourd-muet de naissance* (A Course of Instruction for a Deaf-Mute Born Person). Paris: Le Clere. 580 pages.

Siepmann, Heinrich, and Friedrich Waldow, editors, 1972. Fingeralphabetzeichen für deutsche Buchstaben (Fingerspelling signs for German letters). *Deutsche Gehörlosen-Zeitung* (German Newspapers for the Deaf). 23:49-50. 20 Februar.

Smith, Garth, Ann Kentwell and Ross Dyson, 1978 (?). *Let's Talk with our Hands.* New South Wales, Australia: North Rocks Central School for Deaf Children. 133 pages.

Smith, Wayne H., and Ting Li-fen, eds., 1979. *Shou neng sheng chyau* (Your Hands Can Become a Bridge). 1. English edition. xxxiv and 33 pages. 2. Chinese edition. 282 pages. Peitou, Taipei, Taiwan: The Sign Language Club and the Sign Language Training Classes.

Starcke, Hellmuth, and Günter Maisch, 1977. *Die Gebärden der Gehörlosen* (The Sign Language of the Deaf). Hamburg, West Germany: Pergamos-Druck Heidrich & Bender. 479 pages.

Sternberg, Martin L. A., 1981. *American Sign Language: A Comprehensive Dictionary.* New York: Harper & Row, Publishers. 1132 pages.

Stichting Doof-Blinden, 1979. *Communicatie-mogelijkheden voor doof-blinden* (Communication-possibilities for deaf-blind persons). 's Gravenhage, The Netherlands: Stichting Doof-Blinden (Zichtenburglaan 260; 2544 EB 's Gravenhage). 39 pages.

Stokoe, Jr., William C., Dorothy C. Casterline, and Carl G. Croneberg, 1976. *A Dictionary of American Sign Language on Linguistic Principles.* Silver Spring, Maryland: Linstok Press. New Edition. 346 pages.

Szczepankowski, Bogdan, 1974. *Jezyk Migowy, Czesc II: Daktylografia* (Sign Language. Part II Dactylography). Warsaw, Poland: Zaklad Wydawnictw CRS. 53 pages.

Vasishta, Madan, James Woodward and Susan De Santis, 1981. *An Introduction to Indian Sign Language (Focus on Delhi).* College Park, Maryland: Sign Language Research, Inc. 176 pages.

Venus, Michael, 1826. *Methodenbuch, oder Anleitung zum Unterrichte der Taubstummen* (Methodology, or Introduction to the Education of Deaf-Mutes). Wien: Carl Gerold. 392 pages.

von der Lieth, Lars, 1967. *Dansk Døve Tegnsprog* (Danish Sign Language of the Deaf). Copenhagen, Denmark: Akademisk Forlag. 175 pages.

von Ostermann, Georg F., 1952. *Manual of Foreign Languages.* 4th edition, revised. New York: Central Book Company, Inc. 414 pages.

Weld, Lewis, Principal, 1843. *The 27th Report of the Directors of the American Asylum, at Hartford, for the Education and Instruction of the Deaf and Dumb.* Hartford, Connecticut: Case, Tiffany and Burnham, printers. 51 pages.

Werner, Hans, 1932. *Geschichte des Taubstummenproblems bis ins 17. Jahrhundert* (History of the Problems of the Deaf-Mute until the 17th Century). Jena, Germany: Verlag von Gustav Fischer. 275 pages.

Williams, Job, Principal, 1881. *The 65th Annual Report of the Directors and Officers of the American Asylum at Hartford for the Education and Instruction of the Deaf and Dumb.* Hartford, Connecticut: Press of The Case, Lockwood and Brainard Co. 36 pages.

Yanulob, Nikola, Marcho Radulov and Khristo Georgiev,1961. *Krat'k Mimicheski rechnik* (A Short Handbook of Gestures). Sofia, Bulgaria: Izdatelstvo "Narodna Prosveta". 251 pages.

Yau, S. C., 1977. *The Chinese Signs: Lexicon of the Standard Sign Language for the Deaf in China.* Paris, France: Editions Languages Croises. 121 pages.

de Yebra, Melchor, 1593. *Libro llamado refugium infirmorum . . . (A Refuge for the Infirm).* Madrid: Luis Sanchez.

Zhou, Youguang, 1980. The Chinese finger alphabet and the Chinese finger syllabary. *Sign Language Studies* 28:209-216.

INDEX OF COUNTRIES

NOTES